The Joy of Laziness

The Joy of Laziness

How to slow down and live longer

Dr Peter Axt
Dr Michaela Axt-Gadermann

BLOOMSBURY

DUMFRIES & GALLOWAY COLLEGE

A BLOOMSBURY REFERENCE BOOK
Created from the Bloomsbury Business Database
www.ultimatebusinessresource.com

© Bloomsbury Publishing Plc 2005
© F.A. Herbig Verlagsbuchhandlung GmbH, München 2003
© Peter Axt and Michaela Axt-Gadermann 2003

First published in Germany in 2001 by F.A. Herbig Verlagsbuchhandlung GmbH as
Vom Glück der Faulheit.

First published in English in 2003 by Hunter House, Inc., Publishers, USA, as
The Joy of Laziness.

First published in Great Britain by
Bloomsbury Publishing Plc
38 Soho Square
London W1D 3HB

British Library Cataloguing in Publication Data
A CIP record for this book is available from the British Library.

ISBN 0–7475–7676–9
Design by Fiona Pike, Pike Design, Winchester
Typeset by RefineCatch Limited, Bungay, Suffolk
Printed in Italy by Legoprint

All papers used by Bloomsbury Publishing are natural, recyclable products made from wood grown in well-managed forests. The manufacturing processes conform to the environmental regulations of the country of origin.

Contents

Foreword

by Professor Cary Cooper

The Red Queen in Lewis Carroll's *Through the Looking Glass* reflected:

> 'A slow sort of country! Now here, you see, It takes all the running you can do, to keep in one place. If you want to get somewhere else, you must run at least twice as fast as that!'

This aptly describes where we are going in the United Kingdom and most of the developed world. We are working longer hours, under more pressure and leading a pace of life that leaves us at breaking point. Indeed, one of the overriding sources of stress for many people is constant, unrelenting, and largely unpredictable change. This has many significant consequences, but surely one of the most challenging is the fact that jobs are no longer for life – job security is a vestige of the past as organisations now expect their employees to be more adaptable, self-motivated, diligent, loyal, and effective. At the same time, employers offer little or no guarantee of job security, while career development opportunities ebb and flow with economic and business cycles. These constantly shifting job demands and career expectations require personal adjustment: the onus for ensuring health, wealth, and happiness now rests with the individual completely. This requires greater self-initiative and control, but it need not be another source of stress. The *joy* of laziness is being able to accomplish as much or more than you do at present but in a way that leaves you feeling more satisfied, happier, and less stressed.

Stress, this six-letter word, has found a firm place in our modern vocabularies. We throw the term about casually to describe a wide range of ills resulting from our hectic pace of life. 'I really feel stressed,' someone says to describe a vague yet often acute sense of discomfort and lack of tranquillity. It is sometimes hard to know when one is suffering from stress – or the danger of it – because it invariably builds up gradually over time and is all-consuming, being difficult to separate from normal behaviour. Stress is a personal matter, and the symptoms can be behavioural, physical, or both. What causes stress for you and those close to you? How do you react – and above all, how could you improve the situation, permanently?

The issue of stress is one that has finally become acknowledged and accepted in the modern workplace, and with this has come recognition of the sources of stress. Whilst some controlled measure of stress is actually useful – ensuring that concentration is heightened and performance improved accordingly – the consequences of stress are particularly important as it reduces personal effectiveness, saps morale, and clouds judgment. For these reasons and many others, people need to be able to manage their own personal stress and reduce the level and incidence of stress in others. An ability to work hard is seen as being entirely virtuous, the defining characteristic of successful, respected people. Unfortunately, this mindset can lose sight of the importance of balance, the need to work 'smart', and to look after oneself.

The Joy of Laziness is the antidote to a stressful way of life. It is not really about being lazy but about finding the right balance in your life. It is about taking care of yourself, conserving your energy, having periods of peace and recuperation, about eating well, about sleeping well – about 'getting a life'. It is worth reflecting on the words of US actress and comedienne, Lily Tomlin:

'The trouble with being in the rat race is that even if you win, you're still a rat.'

The Joy of Laziness is full of helpful tips to ensure better balance, includes simple but meaningful proverbs on life, questionnaires for self evaluation, but most important of all, it is positive and orientated towards helping the individual to take responsibility for his or her own lifestyle.

This book is as entertaining and thought-provoking as it is helpful. It shows you how to live a more relaxed life, explaining issues such as:

★ how much energy each person has in his or her 'lifetime account'
★ why lazy people live longer
★ why relaxing makes you cleverer
★ why being lazy strengthens your immune system
★ how you can avoid tension and stress

In the 1970s, Studs Terkel suggested in his acclaimed book *Working: People Talk About What They Do All Day and How They Feel About What They Do*, a collection of hundreds of interviews with working people from all walks of life, that:

'work is about a search for daily meaning as well as daily bread, for recognition as well as cash, for astonishment rather than torpor, in short, for a sort of life rather than a Monday through Friday sort of dying.'

This wonderful book is in the same tradition, not so much about learning how to be lazy but how to 'live' life to its full. I strongly recommend it to all those who want better balance.

Cary Cooper CBE is professor of organisational psychology and health at Lancaster University Management School.

Introduction

'Good health is a present you must give yourself'
— Bodo Werner

Do you believe you need to maintain an intense fitness regime to live longer?

Do you think that getting up early is a sign of dynamic living and vitality?

Do you advocate the view that professional success is impossible without a ten-hour workday?

Do you still think it's healthy to sleep in a cold bedroom?

Do you believe it's beneficial to eat five small meals a day?

Forget it! Recent scientific research indicates that in the future we will need to rethink our attitudes completely if we want to become healthy, successful, and productive in the long term.

In researching our book *Just Stay Young*, we came across facts that called into question countless theories about success, productivity, and health. Excessive athletic ambition, cold morning showers, and getting up early actually seem to be detrimental to a long, healthy life. Again and again, we met older but hearty and active people who didn't meet standard expectations for healthy behaviour. At first we thought that good genes were responsible for their exemplary health and fitness. This was not the case. The parents of the subjects in this group were no more long-lived than the parents of their fitness- and health-conscious peers. But the long-lived subjects had definite advantages over other people: they were calm in every situation, they enjoyed life, played sports – if at all – in moderation, ate little, and did not waste their valuable life energy. Excessive ambition was foreign to them. This approach to life seems to be the secret to vitality and good health.

In light of our research and current scientific findings, we have developed a programme that will help you achieve health and well-being in an enjoyable way, while giving you a good chance of staying young longer.

The wonderful and amazing thing about this programme is this: you can finally, with a clear conscience, do what you have never dared to do – relax and do nothing for a change! For the first time, you're being given scientifically grounded arguments telling you why it's all right to be lazy every so often; why too much exercise will make you sick; why late sleepers live longer; how you can become more intelligent and healthier by being relaxed and even-tempered; and why going south for winter holidays can give you a longer life.

— Peter Axt and Michaela Axt-Gadermann

Important Note

The material in this book is intended to provide a review of natural therapies. Every effort has been made to provide accurate and dependable information. However, you should be aware that professionals in the field may have differing opinions and change is always taking place. If any of the treatments described herein are used, they should be undertaken only under the guidance of a licensed health-care practitioner. The author, editors, and publishers cannot be held responsible for any error, omission, professional disagreement, outdated material, or adverse outcomes that derive from use of any of these treatments in a programme of self-care or under the care of a licensed practitioner.

Chapter One

A mouse has as much life energy as an elephant

1

*'There is nothing humans want to preserve more, yet cultivate less,
than their health.'*

— Jean de la Bruyère (1645–1696), French moralist

This chapter covers:
- ★ why we must do 'nothing' in order to stay healthy and fit
- ★ why animals live longer in the zoo
- ★ how much energy each person has in his or her lifetime account
- ★ which markers of longevity you should watch

Not everyone looks their age

Recently, a patient came into my (Dr Michaela Axt-Gadermann) dermatology practice to get some advice regarding a skin problem before her trip to the Philippines. At first I thought my assistant had given me the wrong patient's notes. I'd estimated the woman's age to be about 65, but according to the information on her card she was already 84. Since I'm always interested in finding out 'secret recipes' for staying young, I naturally asked what her method was for looking so youthful, and for her apparent vitality and good health. 'I don't know exactly, of course,' she responded, 'but since my marriage at 31, my husband and I have fasted one day a week. I've also always tried to keep calm and relaxed in all situations.' She'd never done any sports. 'On the contrary, I'm actually pretty lazy and I like to lie in.' This 'secret recipe' was nothing spectacular, I thought at first. Since then, I've realised it's sensational.

You yourself have probably realised, more than once in your life,

3

that you've completely misjudged a person's age. If you're only a year or two off, others can usually accept it. Your mistake is within the bounds of tolerance. It's more embarrassing when you mistakenly judge a person to be ten or more years older. In these cases, you often excuse yourself by saying that you're a bad judge of age, and that's why you were mistaken. It's more likely, however, that you've made no mistake at all, and that you've correctly established the person's age on the basis of his or her appearance and behaviour. All of us have, in the course of our lives, saved the images of people and their accompanying ages in our brains. When we encounter another person, our brain – much like a computer – calculates the average of these saved images and compares this value to the appearance of the new person, all within a split second. Our ability to judge the age of another person depends heavily on this experiential data and can vary widely from the person's actual age. A person's appearance, however, often gives us important information about his or her biological (functional) age. Someone whose age is often underestimated is usually in better shape and is biologically younger than his or her contemporaries. Fortunately, the speed at which one ages isn't inevitable. The tempo of the ageing process can be influenced. With our programme, you have the potential to let your biological clock run a little slower, helping you stay young longer. If, however, you continue to live like most of your peers, you'll age like them too.

How you may age if you don't change your life

Around the age of 25:
Your muscles' ability to react is decreasing imperceptibly.

Around the age of 30:
The first lines become visible around your eyes. Your bones have reached their maximum strength, and from now on bone density decreases. Men notice that their hair is thinning.

Around the age of 35:

Your hearing is a little worse, but in most cases you don't notice it because the ability to hear high-pitched sounds goes first.

Around the age of 40:

Heart function decreases after age 40. For men, testosterone levels decrease by approximately 1% every year. It also becomes harder to read the newspaper. You have to hold the paper further and further away in order to focus on the small print – this is the first sign of long-sightedness. Perhaps you already need reading glasses.

Around the age of 45:

If you're a woman, you're probably entering menopause now. Your body produces fewer hormones. Bone density is decreasing rapidly.

If you're a man, you may notice that the bald spots on your head are spreading, while body hair is noticeably thicker. Diminished testosterone is largely responsible for these changes.

For both sexes: calorie requirements are much lower. You gain weight as muscles are replaced by fat.

Around the age of 50:

Your ability to process oxygen decreases. Circulation grows worse.

Ages 60 to 70:

Short-term memory function decreases. You can still recite the poems you learned at school, but sometimes forget where you put your car keys. In addition, your immune system isn't as effective as it used to be, and colds last longer. Your sense of balance decreases. Approximately one in three women and one in five men suffer from osteoporosis, or decreased bone density. One in three people has clogged arteries. Since the age of 20, your muscle mass has decreased by 11 to 20 lbs (5 to 9 kg).

HOW YOUR ORGANS TELL YOUR AGE[1]			
	AGE 25	AGE 45	AGE 65
Heart function	100%	94%	81%
Lung capacity	100%	82%	62%
Cholesterol level	198 mg/dl	221 mg/dl	224 mg/dl
Muscle strength	100%	90%	75%
Kidney function	100%	88%	69%

You must do 'nothing' in order to stay healthy and fit

Every organism ages over the course of its life. That cannot be changed. You can, however, influence the speed at which your ageing progresses. What do you have to do in order to put the brakes on ageing? You may be surprised to learn that we aren't recommending an extreme fitness programme, sending you to a plastic surgeon, or prescribing hormone treatments. Until now, you've undoubtedly received quite different answers to these questions. You may have been of the opinion that getting through a triathlon was the key to good health and resilience, and that a ten-hour working day was the only way to achieve professional success and societal recognition.

We, on the other hand, are advising composure, contentedness, moderation, and even occasional indolence if you want to be healthy, productive, and successful. Contentedness and moderation do not mean that you have to be contented with mediocre things and unsatisfactory situations. What we mean is that you should avoid extremes in all areas of your life. Extreme sports, excessive eating, and false ambition are factors that can steal our energy, cause us to age faster, and shorten our lives.

'Never be afraid to sit awhile and think', advised the playwright Lorraine Hansberry (1939–1965). Do not be afraid of peace and quiet, of doing nothing, of laziness, or inactivity – for during this seemingly unproductive time you're doing something wonderful for your body: you're saving energy.

In 1908, a German physiologist, Max Rubner (1854–1932), determined that every organism is provided with a limited amount of life energy. This theory was, however, forgotten, and only in recent years has it been brought back to our attention. In the latter half of the twentieth century, Roland Prinzinger continued research on the life energy theory – officially known as the Metabolic Theory – and determined that apparently all forms of life have the same amount of life energy, dependent on body weight. According to his calculations, each organism can use approximately 2,500 kilojoules of energy per gram of body weight. Roy Walford, a well-known American researcher of the ageing process confirms this finding. (He was the physician living inside Biosphere 2 for two years and has written several books on diets for longer life.) He adds, however, that human beings are much better off than most animals in this respect. According to his calculations, a human being has about twice as much life energy per unit of body weight.[2]

In other words, each of us begins life with a calorie and energy account we can draw on in the years to come. Sooner or later – depending on our lifestyle – the account is used up. Unfortunately, there's no overdraft protection on this life energy account. It's up to us whether we will travel thriftily through life or rush through it wastefully.

Good health and longevity, according to this theory, are above all dependent on the speed with which the metabolism takes in the nourishment we give it and converts it into energy. If we succeed in lowering our metabolic rate, and thereby our consumption of energy, we will age more slowly. The result: a long and healthy life. Energy consumption is largely dependent on our lifestyle. Every day we encounter countless energy thieves. Stress, frustration, cold temperatures, sleep deprivation, poor nutrition, and an inappropriate fitness regimen are among these. High energy use accelerates the ageing process, makes us more susceptible to illness and can even shorten our lifespan. If, on the other hand, we use our energy reserves wisely – by taking various measures to decrease our metabolic activity – we'll be healthier and more productive.

Energy-conserving fruit flies live longer . . .

Fruit flies are the pets of genetic researchers, since the insects' genes are particularly easy to test. Additionally, the flies' short lifespan is practical for researchers of longevity because it makes quick research results possible.

At first glance, these fruit flies (*Drosophila*) have nothing in common with us, but in many cases the discoveries made about fruit flies can lead to conclusions about human processes. Nearly 80% of *Drosophila*'s genome (the entirety of their genes) is the same as that of human beings.

Recently, researchers at the University of Connecticut in Farmington discovered a genetic mutation in fruit flies that allows them to live twice as long as their counterparts. The mutation, which scientists have christened 'Indy' – an acronym in homage to the film *Monty Python and the Holy Grail*, in which a person suffering from the bubonic plague calls out 'I'm not dead yet!' while he's carted away with the deceased – has a direct correlation with the animals' energy use and metabolism.

Dr David Finkelstein of the National Institute on Aging in the United States comments: 'What is interesting . . . is the recurrence of the link between metabolism, caloric restriction, and longevity. This study points to the possibility that if you genetically alter metabolism, you can alter lifespan.'

. . . and it's similar for women

Everywhere in the world, regardless of a country's form of civilisation, and of individuals' nutrition and societal position, women live longer than men. On average, they live five to eight years longer. Is this because of hormones, better nutrition, or just their constitutions? Scientists are undecided. We're of the opinion that women's higher life expectancy has to do with their energy-saving metabolism. A woman's conversion rate is about 10% lower than that of a man of the same size and weight. This means that a woman uses 10% less life energy than a man in the same amount of time. What is interesting in this context is that – independent of the average life expectancy in each country – women live about 10% longer than men.

Size isn't an issue when it comes to a creature's amount of life energy

Small, light animals generally have a very active metabolism, evidenced by a fast heartbeat and a high breathing rate. This uses up a lot of calories, of course, so these organisms use their allotted energy very quickly. A mouse, then, will live to be about four years old, a chimpanzee to be 50, an elephant to be 70, and a turtle to be about 150. All of them have used up approximately the same amount of life energy per gram of body weight. Organisms with a lower energy conversion rate are more careful with their energy reserves than those with comparatively high energy use, especially slow and inactive animals. Turtles, for example, which aren't agitated by anything, live noticeably longer since they waste the least amount of 'life energy'. A similar example is the queen bee. Slothful and generally inactive, she sits in the beehive and is waited on by her worker bees. Her laziness makes it possible for her to live for five or more years. The industrious worker bees, however, use up their life energy within three to six months.

Life expectancy is especially high in a zoo

This theory is confirmed by a comparison of animals in the wild with animals in captivity. In the Serengeti, lions live only eight to ten years. Lions in the zoo, on the other hand, can live to be 20 years old. Polar bears in the Arctic do not generally live longer than 20 years, while in captivity they live up to 40 years. Of course, medical care is better in a zoo than in the wild, but the main contrast is the different way of life. While wild animals cover many miles daily in search of food, and consequently are under a great deal of stress, zoo animals lead a very restful and relaxed life. Their range of movement – which critics often note as a negative aspect of zoo life – is at a minimum; no unnecessary energy is used in searching for food and there are no natural enemies to cause the animals any stress.

Zoo animals are only rarely exposed to energy-robbing situations. The result is a longer life.

HOW LONG HUMAN BEINGS AND ANIMALS CAN LIVE (ESTIMATED MAXIMUM LIFE EXPECTANCY)

worker bee	3–6 months	dolphin	30 years
mole	2 years	bat	30 years
mouse	4 years	brown bear	47 years
queen bee	5–20 years	chimpanzee	50 years
inchworm	6 years	ostrich	62 years
dog	18 years	alligator	66 years
snail	18 years	owl	68 years
cat	20 years	elephant	70 years
lion in the wild	10 years	eagle	80 years
lion in captivity	20 years	freshwater mussel	100 years
polar bear in the wild	20 years	human being	130 years*
polar bear in captivity	40 years	turtle	150 years

*Most anti-ageing experts believe that the maximum life expectancy for a human being under ideal conditions is 120 to 130 years. This life expectancy is based on numerous studies by Hayflick and others. It's estimated that 50% of our life expectancy is determined by genes, and that we can influence the other 50% with our lifestyle (nutrition, stress reduction, etc).

Living by the Formula-1 principle – maximum power and a short lifespan

Every driver knows which driving techniques can ruin his or her engine and which can lengthen the vehicle's lifespan. Formula-1 racing cars are full of power, impressive, and fast. Their drivers push them to the limits of their capability. After a race of about 155 miles (250 km), they're used up; the engines must be completely overhauled.

Diesel engines aren't among the most dynamic modes of transportation, but it doesn't make a big difference to their owners that the engines are generally somewhat more leisurely and sluggish than those that run on petrol. In exchange, they easily reach several hundred thousand miles when driven carefully. After all, diesel lorries are so slow that other drivers get upset about them. But they can cover more than 600,000 miles (up to a million km) without any engine trouble.

The human body works according to a similar principle. It's up to us whether we protect our bodies and use our resources responsibly or use up our energy in a short amount of time. Most people, it seems, believe they have to live according to the Formula-1 principle, and they even receive societal recognition for doing so. Not only workers, but also retired people and schoolchildren now run around with packed schedules. Those who manage to make countless professional and social appointments daily are admired. When someone says that they've worked 70 hours over the past week, we see them as successful. If someone else says, halfway through the year, that they don't have a single day free for the rest of the year, we conclude that they're not only professionally, but also socially respected. A mobile phone that is always on is seen as a status symbol, and anyone who isn't reachable at every hour of the day believes he or she is missing something important. We are perpetually active, but often only occasionally effective, and we're wasting valuable life energy on unimportant things.

It's easy to recognise people who live according to the Formula-1 principle:

★ They always want to be the winner, at work and in their free time.
★ They place professional success ahead of family and friends.
★ They always have to be right.
★ They cannot delegate but must control everything.
★ They must spend every minute of the day 'constructively' and never have any time to relax.
★ They always want to have everything and cannot be satisfied with some of it.
★ They seem careless of their energy.

'The Indispensable One'

Unfortunately, over time we've forgotten how to let go of the tasks – ultimately insignificant to our lives – that place undue stress on us and require much of our time and energy. We've forgotten how to concentrate only on the truly important things. As a result, we're placed in unnecessarily stressful situations; we lose our composure, rob our bodies of important life energy, and may even be shortening our lives. This point is illustrated clearly by the story of Kevin B., a lawyer. Kevin B. was there for his clients day and night. He helped everyone who asked him for advice and was heavily involved as one of the representatives of his riding club. His days were booked from Monday through to Sunday, often until late at night. Allegedly, he could get by on five to six hours of sleep a night. He was even proud that he didn't have to 'waste' his time on such unimportant things as sleep. If he was sleepy during the day, he replenished his spirits with a couple of cups of coffee. He tried to battle his constant daily stress with food, and as a result he was overweight. He had hardly any free time. The time he spent with his family was short and carefully measured. The family allowed themselves a holiday only once a year – but even here the lawyer believed he had to show great accomplishments. He wanted to be the best on the tennis and squash courts, and was always the leader on their hikes. He believed he was doing something good for his health and thereby combatting his stress at work. At the age of 51, he decided to take a partial retirement from his practice in order to spend more time with his family and friends. He looked for a partner who could take on some of his work, but this never happened. Kevin B. died of a heart attack.

We can't know for sure exactly what led to his heart attack, but one of the likely causes was the cumulative stress under which he lived. It's entirely possible that he had used up his supply of life energy prematurely.

Several thousand people came to his funeral. The eulogies were full of praise. It seemed that the gap he'd left in public life could never be filled. Today, half a year later, his name – except within his family – is already almost forgotten.

> *Wherever action could be found,*
> *he was there, he was around;*
> *nothing could be done without him,*
> *not one hour had he free.*
> *Yesterday, when he was buried,*
> *he was there too, naturally.*
> — Wilhelm Busch, from 'The Indispensable One'.[3]

Rediscovering relaxation

Most people's goals include being healthy, young, vital, and success-ful. In a representative poll of German citizens taken for *Stern* magazine in 1998–99, 98% of people aged 18 to 70 said that health was 'very' or 'somewhat' important to them. According to a Gallup

Poll from 2003, 'Americans rate family and health as the two most important aspects of their lives.'[4]

Even if health seems to be the most important thing for most people, it's probably the aspect attended to least. Nowadays we connect stress, a hectic schedule, and constant activity with success, good health, fitness, and productivity.

This way of thinking has caused us to forget the qualities most important to staying healthy in our hectic society: equanimity, calmness, and moderation. These old and apparently unmodern virtues are the real fundamentals for realising our dream of good health.

Unfortunately, when we speak of these virtues, we often make the mistake of associating them only with the mental or spiritual realm. In reality, they are key aspects of our entire lifestyle and should therefore be considered in relation to diet, work, and even physical activity. If you practise these virtues, you'll save important 'life energy', while at the same time improving your chances of having a long life.

There are a variety of ways that we waste valuable life energy, including the following:

★ through stress
★ through cold
★ through movement
★ through lack of sleep
★ through eating
★ through some stimulants

TEST YOURSELF: HOW MUCH ENERGY ARE YOU WASTING?

1 HOW WOULD YOU DESCRIBE YOUR PROFESSIONAL/ PRIVATE STRESS?

a	I feel overworked almost every day.	2 points
b	Stressful phases are balanced with calm phases.	1 point
c	Can't complain about stress.	0 points

2 WHICH SENTENCE BELOW BEST DESCRIBES THE RELATIONSHIP BETWEEN YOUR WEIGHT AND THE TYPE AND QUANTITY OF FOOD YOU CONSUME?

a	I overeat and I'm overweight.	2 points
b	I can eat as much as I want without gaining weight.	2 points
c	My weight is normal/ideal, but I have to watch what I eat in order to maintain my weight.	0 points

3 DO YOU SMOKE?

a	Yes, I smoke a pack a day.	1 point
b	Yes, I smoke more than a pack a day.	2 points
c	No.	0 points

4 DO YOU EXERCISE?

a	Yes, I exercise up to four hours a week, divided into three or four sessions.	0 points
b	Yes, I exercise more than four hours a week.	1 point
c	No, I don't exercise.	1 point

5 WHAT TEMPERATURES DO YOU PREFER?

a	I'm very sensitive to cold and prefer warm rooms. I tend to wear warm clothing.	0 points
b	I prefer to stay in cold rooms and wear relatively thin clothing.	1 point
c	I think I have a normal 'thermostat'.	0 points

6 HOW MANY CUPS OF COFFEE, BLACK TEA, OR OTHER CAFFEINATED BEVERAGES DO YOU DRINK DAILY?

a	I don't drink any.	0 points
b	I drink one to two drinks a day.	1 point
c	I drink more than two drinks a day.	2 points

7 HOW MUCH DO YOU GENERALLY SLEEP?

a	I sleep less than seven hours.	2 points
b	I sleep seven to eight hours.	1 point
c	I sleep more than eight hours.	0 point

Calculating your score

0–4 points: Congratulations! You're already living according to the energy-saving principle. However, you'll probably find even more recommendations for conserving energy in our book – so it's worthwhile for you to keep reading.

5–8 points: Be careful; in some areas of your life you're wasting energy unnecessarily. Go through the test again, paying special attention to the answers that gave you two points. This is where you have the potential to save a lot of energy by changing your lifestyle. The suggestions in this book for saving energy will be helpful to you.

9–14 points: You're living by the Formula-1 principle, and throwing your energy out the window in several areas of your life. Put on the brakes – the following tips and programmes can help you. You'll find that you benefit from our recommendations even after a short amount of time.

Protect yourself from energy thieves

Life energy is a calculable energy – that is, it's an identifiable number of calories. Many factors contribute to the depletion of energy reserves over the course of a lifetime. Everyone knows that movement uses up calories, and therefore energy. Less well known is that stress, too, increases calorie use. The stress hormones adrenaline and noradrenaline (also known as epinephrine and norepinephrine), found in the bloodstream, are multiplied by stress and increase metabolism – and thereby energy use – by up to 15%. Mental stress leads to physical stress. Contracted muscles use up additional calories. Amazingly, even eating can steal energy: depending on the food we take in, our bodies require more or less energy to process it. Getting up early is often seen as a sign of a dynamic lifestyle, but every hour less that we sleep costs us approximately 50 calories of life energy. Cold showers, cool rooms, and special spa treatments are thought to harden our bodies. In reality, however, these measures stimulate metabolism, and thereby increase energy use. You see, therefore, that there are numerous ways to waste or save energy. It's possible to conserve energy in many everyday situations. Of all these, the most important steps to take for your energy-saving programme are the following large and small energy-savers:

Large energy-savers:
★ Maintain calm and even-temperedness in all areas of life.
★ Be moderate in eating.
★ Be moderate in exercise.

Small energy-savers:
★ Decrease energy use through heat management.
★ Sleep longer.
★ Avoid stimulants that increase energy use.

If you follow as many of these recommendations as possible, you'll be saving important life energy. The three big energy-savers are the foundation of our programme, since they make it relatively easy to save large amounts of energy. The smaller energy-savers provide very good support for the programme. Very few people will be able to make changes in every area of their lives right away. Instead, look for an area of your life in which it will be fairly easy for you to make changes. Eventually you'll be able to broaden your energy-saving programme more and more. Since the energy saved from each area is cumulative, it's probably easier for most of us to make moderate changes in several areas than extreme changes in one area.

This isn't all, though. The behaviour mentioned above is related to further changes which can be determined subjectively and measured objectively. After a short amount of time, you'll probably feel physically and mentally better. These positive changes are objectively measurable. They're important evidence of an improved physical state, and probably also an indication of your functional age. Several years ago, a German doctor named Franke determined that the cholesterol levels, blood sugar levels, etc of healthy hundred-year-olds were much lower than would be expected, while those of invalids in the same age range were clearly deviant from the norm, experiencing 'age-typical' changes.[5]

We've compiled the measurements that are useful in indicating your vitality, health, and biological age.

Take our word for it: the following measurements are good for your health

We promise that you'll not only feel better if you follow our recommendations, but that you'll actually become healthier and more productive. From the fields of sports and medicine we have learned some simple tests that will give you a very good indication of the state of your fitness and health. Some of these tests you can do yourself, others you should have done by your doctor. We will explain how these measurements are related to your productivity and health. In our research, we noticed that parameters like cholesterol level, stress-hormone level, productivity, blood sugar, and blood pressure aren't affected solely by what we eat. Relaxation, sufficient sleep, warmth, sunlight, and moderate movement can have positive effects on many of these blood levels.

ACTIONS THAT HAVE A POSITIVE EFFECT ON YOUR HEALTH INDICATORS	
ACTION YOU CAN TAKE	HEALTH INDICATOR OR PARAMETER THAT IS POSITIVELY AFFECTED
moderation in eating	weight, blood pressure, blood sugar, blood cholesterol, uric acid, homocysteine, PWC 130*
relaxation and calmness	blood pressure, blood sugar, antibodies (lymphocytes), stress-hormone levels

moderate exercise	weight, stress-hormone levels, PWC 130* (if you weren't exercising before), blood pressure (if you were not exercising before), antibodies
warmth and sunlight	blood sugar level, blood pressure, weight
sufficient sleep	cortisol level, antibodies, blood sugar level

*PWC (Physical Working Capacity) 130 tells you about the working capacity of your circulatory system. PWC 130 is explained on page 18.

In the rest of this chapter you'll learn what each of these levels shows and why it's important to keep your levels within a healthy range.

A	LEVELS YOU CAN CHECK	
1	resting pulse	60 to 70 heartbeats per minute
2	body weight	see Appendix 2
3	blood pressure	systolic to 140/diastolic to 85

B	LEVELS YOUR DOCTOR MUST CHECK FOR YOU:	
4	blood sugar	
	– in blood (on an empty stomach)	up to 100 mg/dl
	– in urine (on an empty stomach)	undetectable
5	blood fats	
	– triglyceride	up to 125 mg/dl
	– cholesterol	up to 200 mg/dl
	– HDL cholesterol	over 50 mg/dl (men), 60 mg/dl (women)
	– LDL cholesterol	up to 125 mg/dl
6	homocysteine	up to 10 μmol/l
7	uric acid	3.5 to 7.0 mg/dl (men), 2.5 to 5.7 mg/dl (women)
8	antibodies	
	– white blood cells (leukocytes)	4000 to 9000 mm^3
	– lymph cells (lymphocytes)	25–40 %
9	stress hormones	
	– cortisol	less than 150 ng/ml

Your long-life markers

1 Body weight: a 'massive' opportunity for your health

Body weight is an important indicator of your fitness level. It can give insight into whether your daily calorie intake is too high, too low, or just right, and it also can give insight into whether your hormone levels, stress levels, and genetic makeup are 'normal' or healthy. Too much weight limits your productivity, can lead to back pain, and puts stress on the heart and circulation.

Please find our weight recommendations in Appendix 2: The proper weight for adults.

2 Blood pressure: arteries in a choke hold

Blood pressure is the pressure that constantly flows through our veins and arteries. A certain amount of pressure is necessary in order to provide all the organs with enough oxygen and nutrients. However, if the pressure is too high, blood-vessel walls can be damaged by the blood rushing by. These damaged spots become attack points for calcium deposits. In the long run, this leads to hard and inelastic arteries, and calcium deposits can make the arteries narrower.

Blood pressure is measured by two numbers. The first indicates systolic pressure, which results from the contraction of the heart muscle. The second value is the diastolic blood pressure, which is the result of the relaxation of the heart muscle.

3 PWC 130: the production value

The PWC 130 (Physical Working Capacity 130) tells you about the working capacity of your circulatory system. The value shows what capacity (in watts) you can reach on a bicycle ergometer when your pulse is at 130 beats per minute. This production must be considered in relation to your weight and gender. Normal values are 1.5 watts per kilogram of body weight in men, 1.25 for women. Men should aim for 2 watts per kilogram, and women should aim for 1.5 watts.

These are the optimal values for our energy-saving programme. Since these values do not represent a maximum production, they're unrelated to age. Younger healthy people can take the test in any well-equipped fitness studio. If you're over 40 or have heart problems, high blood pressure, or diabetes, you should find a doctor to administer the test. Your PWC 130 values will probably improve if you lower your body weight and/or get a little more exercise. In other words, as you become more fit, you produce *more* energy (work more efficiently) while expending *less*. Keep in mind the guidelines of our recommended energy-saving minimal movement programme. The following table shows how to evaluate your working capacity:

EVALUATION SCALE FOR PWC 130 IN WATT/KG

3	2	1	normal value	1	2	3
low production					high production	
MEN:						
<1.0	1	1.25	1.5	1.75	2.0	2.25
WOMEN:						
<0.65	0.85	1.05	1.25	1.45	1.65	1.85

These values are reached by dividing your watt production on a bicycle ergometer at a pulse of 130 bpm, by your body weight (without clothing) in kilograms (1 kg = 2.2 pounds).

4 Blood-fat values: too much fat closes the arteries

Cholesterol is a component of countless animal-based foods. Eggs, cheese, and meat in particular contain high cholesterol, while vegetables are cholesterol free. Cholesterol is necessary in small amounts and is used, among other things, for the production of various hormones. If blood cholesterol is too high, however, it's generally (with a few exceptions) due to poor nutrition. The excess cholesterol is deposited in the blood vessels and can lead to a tightening of the blood vessels and to clogged arteries. Our energy-saving programme makes it easy, in most cases, to bring your blood cholesterol to a safe level.

Triglycerides are a type of fat that also comes in large part from your diet; it's stored as pockets of fat on the hips, rear, and stomach. High triglyceride levels cause a thickening of the blood, which flows more slowly through the veins and increases the risk of heart attack and stroke.

5 Uric acid: danger for your joints

Uric acid is a byproduct of protein metabolism and increases when we eat too much meat, especially offal, and legumes (or 'pulses'). If the uric acid level is too high, crystals build up in our joints, causing a painful attack of gout. Our energy-saving programme will help you lower your uric acid in the long term. It's also important, however, that you give up most meat, alcohol, and legumes, and drink at least 8 cups (4 pints) of water a day. Vegetarians who rely on legumes as a source of protein need not give them up, though, since most uric acid comes from meat (vegetarians generally do not have problems with uric acid).

6 Blood sugar: just because it tastes good doesn't mean it's good for you

The sugar carried in our blood is the source of energy for our bodies. However, this fuel can only be burned in the organs, and it's only with the help of the hormone insulin that sugar gets where it needs to go. If the hormone is missing, blood sugar levels rise. High blood sugar levels, found in people with diabetes, can hurt blood vessels over time. Blood sugar should be at a maximum of 100 mg/dl on an empty stomach.

7 Antibodies: the organism's bodyguards

In addition to red blood cells (erythrocytes) and platelets (thrombocytes), our blood also contains white blood cells (leukocytes). The lymph cells (lymphocytes) also belong to the family of white blood cells. These play an important role in the immune system. Not only do they attack invading germs, but they can also recognise mutated cells and destroy them before they become tumours. In order to ensure the effectiveness of the immune system, the antibodies must be plentiful as well as in optimal functioning condition. Our antibodies can be damaged by stress, physical over-exertion – including excessive exercise – lack of sleep, and use of stimulants, particularly cigarettes. Relaxation, moderate exercise, fasting, and sufficient sleep help to reactivate the immune system.

8 The stress hormone cortisol: protection and threat

Cortisol (cortisone) is a hormone produced by the adrenal glands. Cortisol is released by stress and frees up energy reserves for the coming attack: blood fats are mobilised, blood sugar rises, and infections are repressed. A short-lived increase of this hormone does not harm the body. A constantly raised cortisol level, as occurs with constant stress, will harm the immune system in the long run and increase the body's tendency towards infections and diabetes. Our brains, too, can be damaged by a high concentration of cortisol. Memory in particular appears to suffer from exposure to the hormone. Recent research has shown that after months of stress, the cortisol level does not return to its original point but remains high even when the organism is at rest.

9 Homocysteine tears up the arteries

The protein building block homocysteine, an amino acid, is formed in the body of a person when another amino acid, methionine, is consumed by that person, usually in the form of a food. Methionine can be found in numerous foods, and large quantities are found in meat. After a meal that includes a lot of meat, homocysteine levels rise sharply.

High homocysteine levels cause damage to the inner walls of the blood vessels, activate the formation of blood clots, and increase the risk of heart attack, stroke, premature ageing of the brain, and thrombosis (blood clots in the venous vessels). The main causes of a rise in homocysteine are a diet rich in meat and a low level of vitamins B-6, B-12, and folic acid. A diet rich in vitamin B, one that includes vitamin B supplements, for example, can lower dangerous amino acid levels at an astonishing rate.

Summary

★ Every life form – even a human being – comes into the world with a full energy account. This life energy can be measured in calories per gram of body weight. When the energy is used up, the organism's life ends.

★ Good health and longevity are dependent on the speed with which life energy is consumed; moderate energy consumption leads to health and longer life. This has been confirmed in numerous studies and observations of various animal species. Animals that move little, hibernate, or are subjected to less stress (for example, by living in a zoo as opposed to in the wild), live longer.

★ We human beings, too, are subject to the same laws of moderation. Since we have the power to shape our own lives, it's possible to use our lifestyle to influence the ageing process.

★ Behaviour that speeds up metabolism and increases calorie use shortens the lifespan. On the other hand, behaviour that slows metabolic activity and saves calories has a life-lengthening effect.

★ Metabolism-calming (energy-saving) behaviour includes: calmness, equanimity in any circumstance, occasionally even laziness and indolence, moderation in eating, moderation in exercise, long sleeping, and keeping warm, as well as avoidance of stimulants that can increase energy consumption.

Chapter Two

Conserving energy by doing 'nothing'

2

'You're only here for a short visit. Don't hurry, don't worry.
And be sure to smell the flowers along the way.'
> — Walter C. Hagen (1892–1969), American golfer

This chapter covers:
- ★ why athletes have bad memories
- ★ why bus passengers live longer than bus drivers
- ★ why couch potatoes are energy savers
- ★ whether the fitness craze is worth your while
- ★ why lazy people live longer

The first marathon runner paid with his life

Are you one of those people who think you have to put your body through a strenuous daily regime in order to stay young longer? Perhaps you hope that going for a jog every day will protect you from a heart attack? Or maybe you're of the opinion that regular aerobic exercise will make you healthier?

Numerous current studies appear to contradict these opinions. Ever since the Greek messenger Pheidippides, in 400 BC, ran the 26.16-mile (42.1 km) stretch from Marathon to Athens and ultimately collapsed, dead, in the marketplace, there has been an ongoing debate over the point (or pointlessness) of excessive athleticism.

A somewhat outdated study gave the fitness craze strong support. About 25 years ago, an American doctor named Ralph Paffenbarger began a study on 17,000 male Harvard graduates. He determined that the risk of heart disease sinks dramatically when you burn an extra 2,000 calories per week through physical activity.[6] From that point on, millions of people exerted themselves on treadmills, squash courts, and in gyms, trying to burn off the magical 2,000 calories. Unfortunately, whenever the study was cited, it wasn't mentioned that the Harvard subjects didn't burn the calories just by exercising, but mostly by climbing stairs, gardening, and doing other similar moderate-intensity tasks. It was also forgotten that Paffenbarger saw health improvements after the subjects had burned only 500 extra calories per week, a fact that would make the frantic overexertion of many fitness enthusiasts completely unnecessary.

Bus passengers live longer than bus drivers

Very few of the studies used by the founders of the fitness movement actually had to do with fitness training, aerobics, or cycling. What they mostly investigated were the effects of moderate exercise and everyday physical activity on overall health. In 1953 it was found that the bus passengers on English double-decker buses suffered fewer heart attacks than the bus drivers. What was the reason? Did the passengers, unlike the bus drivers, ride their exercise bikes every evening? No, it was just the 'athletic exertion' of walking, standing up, and occasional stair climbing that gave the passengers their healthy advantage.

Is the fitness craze worthwhile for you?

You've probably heard and read that regular exercise protects you from disease, makes you younger, and lengthens your life. So you go to a gym twice a week, even though you'd rather be working in the garden. In addition, you jog once a week, even though you don't particularly enjoy it. How much do you think you can lengthen your life by exercising several times a week after the age of 20? Will your hard work get you five, six, eight, ten, or more years?

The reality is that a lifetime of athletic activity can lengthen your life by just two years! Living two years longer is certainly a fine and worthwhile goal, but Dr Jacoby, an American heart specialist, has calculated that the time you spend to reach this goal – on the treadmill, at the gym, or on the tennis court – also equals at least two years![7] If you enjoy exercising, the time is certainly not wasted. But if you're innately a couch potato and are only torturing yourself in order to stay healthy and live longer, then you should consider whether or not the effort is worth it for you. After all, exercising at the gym isn't the only thing that's good for your health. Even moderate 'everyday exercise' like gardening, walking the dog, washing windows, or climbing the stairs is enough to stay healthy and fit.

Couch potatoes are energy savers

If you apply the life-energy theory here, hard physical exertion is just a waste of valuable energy reserves anyway. And the fact that there are very few former high-performance athletes over 80 who are still healthy, mentally active, and productive should give obsessive athletes something to think about.

On the other hand, there are countless examples of elderly people who have never done any exercise or have even avoided it. The best-known opponent of exercise is probably former British prime minister Winston Churchill. He's known for the famous saying, 'No sports'. He followed this rule all his life and lived to the age of 91 (1874–1965). Konrad Adenauer was already 73 years old when he became the first chancellor of Germany in 1949. Only 14 years later, when he had reached the advanced age of 87, did he hand the post over to his successor. Coincidentally, he also died at the age of 91 (1876–1967). About Adenauer's athletic exploits, we know only that he regularly played bocce ball (a game very similar to lawn bowls) during his holidays in Cadenabbia.

Another example is Elizabeth, the Queen Mother, who quite possibly never broke a sweat playing sports in her life. But in 2002 she passed away peacefully in her sleep at the grand old age of 101.

Older athletes live with constant stress

Even we – two people who used to be dedicated long-distance runners – are no longer completely convinced that athletic exercise is healthy! In exercise, it doesn't hold true that 'a lot helps a lot'. Exercise, physical labour, and heavy exertion create an 'emergency situation' for the body. In order to complete the tasks we require of it, the body puts the same mechanisms into motion that it does in any other stressful situation. The adrenal glands excrete cortisol in order to prepare enough energy for the physical task. As a result, the blood sugar level rises. Stress hormones like adrenaline and noradrenaline increase the pulse and blood pressure in order to ensure adequate nutrition of the organism even with the increased exertion. Our breathing rate increases in order to pump more oxygen into the body.

If the exertion, and the associated stress to the body, is light and of relatively short duration, and if the body has enough time to regenerate, then there's no damage to it.

Endurance sports, on the other hand, create constant stress episodes and, in the long term, appear to cause changes in the way the organism regulates stress. If practised with a focus on endurance and results, recreational sports even appear to be as damaging as constant stress at work – a conclusion reached by Meermann at the Max Planck Institute for Psychiatry in Munich. The subjects of the study were older marathon runners (average age 55) who had been running marathons for at least ten years and covered between 75 to 90 miles (120 and 150 km) a week when in training. Blood tests showed that the continual intensive physical exertion led to an overproduction of the stress hormone cortisol in the runners' adrenal glands.[8] The natural regulatory cycle, which is meant to prevent a constant production of the hormone, no longer functions in these runners.

Like a defective thermostat that cannot change its setting back to 'normal' despite a high room temperature, marathon runners' reaction mechanism is so damaged that the high levels of cortisol, once caused by the sport, can no longer return to normal.

The hormone-regulating thermostat

The release of cortisol is regulated by a reaction mechanism in the organism that works in a similar way to a heater's thermostat. During times of stress, a particular region of the brain releases the hormone CRH (corticotrophin releasing hormone). This stimulates the production of another messenger substance, ACTH (adreno-cortico-trophic hormone), which causes the adrenal glands to release the stress hormone cortisol. The released cortisol restricts CRH production, thereby preventing further cortisol production. The cortisol turns itself off, protecting the body from damage. Under chronic stress, this regulatory mechanism is disabled. The result is a constant high level of cortisol in the blood.

Constant stress has also been proven to affect the memory. The Max Planck Institute tests found this effect in long-distance runners who are under constant stress. In comparison to the older test subjects, they had significantly worse short-term memories. After half an hour, the physically active subjects were much worse at recalling new terms than the inactive subjects.

Risk factor: exercise

Exercise is clearly no guarantee of good health and a long life. About 25 years ago, a sportswriter named James Fixx infected Americans with running fever with his bestseller *The Complete Book of Running*.

The book was an immediate bestseller in Europe as well. At the time, James Fixx was known as the 'King of Fitness'. Millions of Europeans followed his advice and tried to stay productive and healthy by running. The book's author set a good example, and even at the age of 50 he jogged about 60 miles (100 km) a week. James Fixx died of heart failure at 52 after a 4-mile race. According to K.H. Cooper, a well-known American sports doctor, James Fixx had covered about 37,000 miles (60,000 km) running, and had participated in some 20 marathons in the 17 years before his death.[9]

Fixx isn't a unique case. Endurance athletes do not appear to lengthen their lives significantly through exercise, reaching only average life expectancy, if that. Jack Kelly, brother of Grace Kelly, won a bronze medal in the Olympics for his rowing and suffered the same fate as Fixx. He, too, died of a heart attack. Emil Zatopek, a famous world-class runner and multiple Olympic long-distance champion, known by sports journalists as the 'Czech locomotive' for his unique running style, died at the age of 78, the result of a stroke. Herbert Schade, his German opponent in the 10,000-metre race, only lived to 72. He died of a heart attack. A non-athlete could be expected to live just as long. Vladimir Kuz, former world record holder in the 5,000- and 10,000-metre race, died at 48, also of a heart attack. All these athletes were, in our eyes, extremely fit and capable. Despite their apparently healthy, body-conscious lifestyle, in many cases they didn't even reach average life expectancy. The frightening thing is that their daily athletic training doesn't appear to have given them any health benefits. Especially noteworthy is the fact that these endurance athletes died of diseases that should actually have been prevented by their chosen sport. Generally, running is recommended as protection from heart attack and stroke.

Cooper speculates that endurance sports provide no health benefits after middle age, and possibly even the opposite. He tells of someone who participated in several ultra-long-distance races but had to give up his sport because of heart disease. His coronary arteries were severely calcified.

Daily newspapers constantly report cases of death during exercise. The public takes these reports, unlike those of car accidents, without comment. During the opening ceremonies of the 2000 Olympic Games, for example, a 74-year-old torch bearer called Ron King, died of a heart attack shortly after passing on the Olympic flame.[10] About ten days later, a 58-year-old Danish man and a 38-year-old woman from Panama did not survive the Berlin Marathon. When interviewed, the emergency doctor said, 'Statistically speaking, we have to expect an inevitable death in every five or six races.'[11]

Exercise: how much is too much?

'The dose makes the poison'; even Hippocrates knew this. The saying appears to apply to athletic training as well.

In recent literature, exercise is constantly cited as a protection against cancer. This advice, however, appears to mean only moderate athletic activity. Intensive exercise does not seem to provide any health benefits in this area. In fact, the risk of cancer probably increases as a result of intensive exercise. Polednak proved, in a study of 8,400 Harvard graduates, that those who exercised intensively were more likely to die of tumours than were non-athletes.[12]

Paffenbarger studied 50,000 male Harvard graduates who exercised either more or less than five hours a week.[13] In this study it became apparent that the subjects who exercised more were significantly more likely to contract prostate cancer.

The frequent cases of cancer among relatively young endurance athletes, as reported by K.H. Cooper, are thought-provoking.[14] A good friend of Cooper's died of cancer at the age of 60. He had completed 524 marathons in his life, making him the world record-holder for the most completed marathons. In the meantime, more and more doctors are seeing a connection between over-training and the development of cancer and other diseases.

Of course, these examples cannot conclusively prove that exercise promotes cancer. They do, however, show the dubious value of intensively practised endurance sports and make it clear that you don't have to do performance-oriented sports to protect your health. It's unfortunate, therefore, that the press always reports on athletes with cancer in a way that implies, to the unbiased reader, that the cancer-stricken athlete's continued practice of the sport is what has restored him or her to good health.

What is overlooked is that the athlete was stricken with the illness *during* his or her career as a first-class athlete.

So it was with Lance Armstrong, the winner of the Tour de France in 1999, 2000, 2001, 2002, 2003, and 2004. When Armstrong came down with testicular cancer, he was already one of the world's best cyclists. He was treated by the book, including chemotherapy, and in the end successfully returned to the competitive arena. The real miracle here is that, despite his cancer, Armstrong was able to become a world-class cyclist again.

Performance-oriented exercise: a knockout punch to your immune system?

Does excessive physical exertion, contrary to what is widely believed, promote chronic illnesses like cancer and clogged blood vessels? As yet there's no comprehensive, confirmed data. It's certain, however, that success-oriented sports have a negative effect on the immune system. Many athletes can attest to this; before important tournaments and big competitions, after training camps and intensive phases of preparation, one cold leads to the next, and sprains and injuries mount.

It's been proven in numerous studies that, after endurance competitions, athletes are significantly more likely to be battling sinus infections, sore throats, and bronchitis. This high susceptibility to infection is due to a temporary weakening of the immune system. In addition, previously existing illnesses are more severe when training is resumed before the infection has completely disappeared. In these cases, the danger of myocarditis, a spreading of the infection to the heart, is especially great. In some cases the heart muscle can even be permanently damaged.

The increased cancer rate in performance athletes may also be due to the frequent weakening of the immune system; mutated cells are formed daily in every human body and can develop into cancer. In a majority of these cases, the cell mutations do not pose any danger because they're detected by our immune system and destroyed. If, however, this defence mechanism isn't fully functioning for a long period of time, it can happen that one of these mutated cells slips by the 'immunity controls' and becomes the starting point for a tumour.

Minimal movement for optimal health

'Make haste slowly', said the Roman emperor Augustus, and we'd like to take his advice. We do need a certain, well-measured amount of movement to keep our organs functioning, to keep our immune system strong, and to be at optimal physical and mental capacity. Such an exercise programme does not, however, have anything to do with performance-oriented fitness training and is miles away from being an extreme sport. Numerous studies have shown that a certain amount of movement protects us from circulatory disease and is good for our health. But athletic exercise isn't necessarily what we need. Even our everyday movement – that is, walking the dog, going shopping, climbing the stairs, and mowing the lawn – can be enough. However, anyone who is missing this everyday exercise, for example because of a sedentary job, should have some kind of minimal exercise programme to follow regularly in order to balance it out.

The 'exercise programme' we describe below serves to maintain your organ and muscle function. It should, above all, contribute to your relaxation and not add another stress factor to your life. Pay special attention to our tips for 'relaxed exercise'. Try to move about regularly. If for some reason time is short, you can skip an exercise session rather than stressing out about it (but don't let it become the rule!).

Our minimal programme for fitness and longevity
The programme consists of:

★ a 30-minute brisk walk, taken three to four times a week

or, alternatively:

★ peripatetic meditation – a combined movement and relaxation programme

You should complete the programme with:

★ a 10 to 15-minute muscle-stretching session, which we recommend you do three times a week

---

More time investment and more intensive training aren't necessary for your health. From the perspective of the Metabolic Theory, the programme offers you the optimal requirements for a long and successful life. More exercise is simply unnecessary.

The brisk walk programme

A brisk walk is neither a comfortable stroll nor a racing stride. In intensity, it's somewhere between the two. Additionally, for brisk walking, not just your legs, but also your arms are involved in the movement. With brisk walking, you can improve your endurance and work out your muscles at the same time.

Things you should know about the brisk walk

★ You don't need any expensive equipment for a brisk walk. You simply need good shoes and comfortable clothing.
★ The brisk walk technique is easy to learn: you just have to bend

your arms while walking and close your hands into fists. Now if you forcefully move your arms in the opposite direction of your feet at every step, you've already mastered the technique required for the brisk walk. With the brisk walk, you're working out not only your legs and your circulatory system but also the muscles in your arms, chest, and back.

★ When doing the brisk walk, pay attention to your pulse. The correct pulse should be between 115 and 120 beats per minute.

★ A tip for determining pulse: you can check your pulse at the wrist or at the throat. Right after the brisk walk, check your pulse for 15 seconds and multiply by four to get your beats per minute. Do not go over the upper limit for pulse, which is generally about 120 beats per minute. A pulse-measuring device, which can be bought at any sports store, will let you check your pulse during training as well.

★ Each brisk walk should last for 30 minutes. During this time a beginner may cover 1.25 miles (2 km) and an advanced walker may cover 2.2 miles (3.5 km).

Peripatetic meditation: relaxing while walking around

The Greek word *peripatein* means 'to go for a walk'. Aristotle's students were called peripatetics because he lectured them in a court-yard (*peripatos*) while walking around. Peripatetic meditation can help you train your circulatory system carefully while at the same time relaxing your spirit. This special kind of walking was developed in 1980 by author Peter Axt. At the time, students who were supposed to be learning about the rudiments of running reported that running was not giving them the relaxation they sought. During training, dis-tracting thoughts crowded into their minds, which had a negative impact on the running experience, and sometimes meant they even had to interrupt the run. With a simple trick – the participants were to count their steps while running – the problematic thoughts were halted instantly, the runners' heads were free, a feeling of peace and relaxation settled in, and the run became a positive experience.

Over the years we've fine-tuned this running meditation somewhat and have used it with great success in treating sleep disturbances, stress, high blood pressure, and mental exhaustion.

Things you should know about peripatetic meditation

★ The exertion shouldn't be so great that you do not enjoy the exercise; you shouldn't be torturing yourself or getting too out of breath. (Don't exceed 120 beats per minute – see the earlier section called **The brisk walk programme** on page 36, for tips on how to measure your pulse.) If the body is overexerted, the desired effect – relaxation – will not occur.

★ Choose a relatively level stretch for walking; a hilly landscape will cause a changing intensity in exercise and will distract you from the relaxing rhythm of your movement.

★ Concentrating on your walking pace makes it easier to tune out distracting thoughts. Such monosyllabic mantras as 'om' or 'ra' have been proven to work when thought at each step. The point of concentrating on these mantras is to block the thought process to prevent the temptation to mull over problems or follow distracting trains of thought. Many people who take meditative walks simply repeat the count from one to ten in rhythm with their steps.

The muscle-stretching programme

Stretching exercises maintain your muscles' elasticity and prevent everyday injuries. After the age of 20, we lose elasticity in our tendons and joints. If we don't do anything about it, we grow less and less flexible. The older we get, the more this inflexibility hinders us in our everyday lives. An appropriate stretching programme can help keep up muscle elasticity and flexibility. We've put together a few easy and effective exercises for the important muscle groups. When doing them, please keep the following ground rules in mind:

★ Stretch your muscles only when they're warm. Cold muscles are prone to injury.

★ Stretch slowly and carefully. Never use force to stretch muscles. Stretching exercises should never be painful.

★ Hold each stretch for 30 seconds.

★ Do each exercise twice.

★ While stretching, breathe calmly and regularly. This relaxes your mind as well as your muscles.

★ After each stretching exercise, take a break of about one minute.

THE MUSCLE-STRETCHING PROGRAMME: HOW TO DO IT

1	**STRETCH THE SHOULDER MUSCLES, THE LATERAL BACK MUSCLES, AND THE TRICEPS**
	Stand up straight. Place one hand at the nape of your neck. With the other hand, exert a light pressure on the elbow. Slowly pull this elbow in the direction of the opposite arm. Hold the tension for about 30 seconds. If you're doing the exercise correctly, you'll feel a slight pulling on your triceps (back of upper arm) and on the sides of your back and shoulders. Now do the same exercise with your other arm. Repeat on each side.
2	**STRETCH THE CHEST MUSCLES**
	Stand up straight and stretch both arms out horizontally in front of your chest. Your arms should be parallel to the floor, and palms should face the floor. Bend your elbows and pull your arms back until your elbows are behind your body. Hold this position for about 30 seconds. Return to the starting position and repeat once.
3	**STRETCH THE WRISTS**
	Stretch your arms up over your head and put your palms together in a 'praying' position. Your fingertips will be pointing up. Pull your hands down slowly, directly in front of your body, keeping the fingertips upward, until you feel a slight tension in your wrists and in your lower arms. Hold this position for about 30 seconds, then return to the starting position and repeat.

4	STRETCH THE UPPER THIGHS AND REAR
	Sit up straight in a chair with a backrest. Rest your left foot on the top of your right thigh. Grab your left ankle with one hand and your left knee with the other, and pull your leg carefully towards your body until you feel a slight tension in your upper left thigh and rear. Hold this position for about 30 seconds, then repeat with the other leg. Repeat once more on each side.
5	STRETCH THE UPPER LEG MUSCLES
	Stand in front of a chair with your feet shoulder-width apart. Lean on the back of the chair with your left hand, bend your right leg back, and grab your right toes with your right hand. Slowly and carefully pull your heel towards your rear until you feel a slight tension in your right upper thigh. Hold the position for about 30 seconds, then repeat with the other leg. Repeat once more on each side.
6	STRETCH THE CALVES
	Stand behind a chair with a backrest, and lean on the back with both hands. Stretch your right leg far back with your heel touching the ground. Bend your left leg until you feel a pulling in your right calf. Hold the position for about 30 seconds, then repeat with the other leg. Repeat once more on each side.

Summary

★ Even in exercise, the saying 'the dose makes the poison' holds true; an overdose of exercise can be harmful.

★ Performance-oriented sports are no guarantee of a long life. In fact, they're probably bad for your health. What is certain is that older endurance athletes who practise their sport competitively and train intensively have a decreased short-term memory. In addition, circulation problems, infections, and even cancer develop just as often in those who play a lot of sports as in those who exercise only moderately.

★ Moderate exercise is still important for our health. A little bit of exercise keeps our organs functioning and our immune system strong. Everyday activities are probably enough.

★ For anyone whose job or lifestyle requires that they sit a lot, we recommend our brisk walk programme and peripatetic meditation.

DUMFRIES & GALLOWAY COLLEGE

Chapter Three

Eat little – live longer

3

'When I go to the market, I realise how many things there are that I don't need.'

— Socrates (*c.* 469–399 BC), Greek philosopher

This chapter covers:
- ★ **how food steals your life energy**
- ★ **what 'breakfast or dinner cancelling' means**
- ★ **how larks and owls need to eat**
- ★ **why fasting makes you younger**

He who gains weight quickly, lives longer

Not everyone uses nourishment equally well. Someone who gains weight just by looking at a piece of cake is, of course, upset about his or her slow metabolism. But these people probably have the best prerequisites for a long life.

Until now, you probably envied those who could eat whatever they wanted and stay thin. In contrast to the good 'food converters' who absorb every calorie of a food – and therefore gain weight faster – thin people generally have a very active metabolism. They burn up their life energy faster. The prerequisite for a long life, however, appears to be a slower metabolism. Even though diets and calorie charts tell us that cutting back on a certain number of calories can help us lose a certain amount of weight, reality is very different. In fact, the metabolic situation is different for everyone. A person with a slower metabolism often has much more trouble losing weight. But this kind of person can save life energy very easily because his or her body is extremely cautious with its energy reserves. This does not, of course, mean that they can eat whatever they want. Just the opposite. Someone who processes food energy well can get by with a significantly reduced number of calories.

If you want to save life energy, though, you must avoid being overweight, whether you have a slow or a fast metabolism. Excess weight indicates that the body is taking in more calories than it needs. Being overweight isn't only a risk factor in the development of numerous organism-ageing diseases such as high blood pressure, diabetes, and clogged arteries; the work of digestion also wastes life energy, and the stored fat is like an overstuffed, heavy backpack that must be carried around day in and day out.

Food costs us energy

At first, it doesn't seem to make sense that food uses up energy. Don't we eat in order to provide the body with energy? But even the digestive process is 'work' for the body, which is why a relatively large percentage of the calories taken in during eating are used for processing the food. One could conclude that easily digestible carbohydrates, which 'waste' less digestive energy, keep us young longer. Hard-to-digest foods like fats and proteins, on the other hand, steal our 'life energy'.

Franke, a researcher of the ageing process from Würzburg, studied the eating habits of healthy 100-year-olds and determined that most of these healthy old people had been moderate eaters their whole lives and generally, with a few exceptions, had been thin. 'The calorie intake of these elderly people . . . varies between about 1,200 and 1,900 calories a day.'[15] In addition, these 'fit old people' said they had avoided gassy, heavy, and sour foods all their lives. They had mostly eaten only easily digestible foods. It's possible that they conserved energy simply through their eating habits, thereby laying the groundwork for a long life.

Recently Dr Paula S., a very healthy 92-year-old doctor and reader of our book *Just Stay Young*, shared with us her secret recipe for a long and healthy life. She wrote, 'You asked about my recipe for staying fit. I don't smoke and don't drink alcohol, and I don't eat much, often only twice a day.' Her only exercise was going on walks; among Franke's subjects, too, none were athletes, but instead did intellectual work or light to moderately heavy manual labour.

Eating less, living longer

Please note: Good health requires that a certain number of calories be taken in; the goal of fasting isn't to lose weight, but to slow the metabolism. If you're underweight, please do not fast without consulting a doctor.

Newspapers, television, and the Internet constantly tell us about new ways to stay young and lengthen our lives. Certainly there are some examples of the promised results, but very few of these methods are scientifically proven. The only method that's proven to slow the ageing process and lengthen the lives of all mammals, including human beings, is a reduction of energy use and a slowing of the metabolism by restricting calorie intake. Countless studies support this finding.

Even in the 1930s, an American researcher named McCay was able to lengthen the lives of rats by more than 50%, simply by reducing their calorie intake. The longest-lived rat in this experiment lived to be 1,800 days old, or 4.9 years. (This corresponds to a human age of about 200 years.) Rats placed on a regular diet lived an average of three years.[16]

The American ageing-process researcher Roy Walford came to a similar conclusion. In studies of human beings, as well as mice, rats, and monkeys, Walford found numerous indications that eating less can lengthen lifespan. Because of this, he recommends lean eating as a recipe for staying young. He first tested this theory successfully on mice. Those mice that were put on a reduced-calorie diet, getting up to 40% less food than their neighbours, lived twice as long as their well-nourished companions. The mice that were allowed to eat as much as they wanted grew weak more quickly, their fur grew dull, and their skin wrinkled – typical signs of ageing. The slim 'hungry mice', on the other hand, kept their shiny coats, stayed agile, and had quick reflexes.[17]

In the meantime, many research teams have broadened their studies to include primates, as they're much more similar to us than rodents. Since they live considerably longer than mice, however, it will be a while before the research can be conclusively analysed. Still, there are a few interesting results so far.

Since 1989, 30 rhesus monkeys have been examined regularly at the University of Wisconsin as part of a 'life-lengthening project'. Half of the subjects are allowed to eat as much as they want while the other half receives about 70% as many calories. The research team has been able to determine that monkeys with reduced calorie intake show signs of rejuvenation similar to those the rodents exhibited. In the 'dieting monkeys', blood sugar levels and levels of insulin, a blood-sugar-lowering hormone, were much lower than in the control group.

This discovery is significant in connection with the ageing process because for all life forms – including human beings – high blood sugar means an increased risk of arteriosclerosis, heart attack, stroke, and other age-related complications. The normally fed monkeys experienced typical age-related changes in certain blood levels. These included a decrease in levels of the so-called antioxidative enzymes. Among other things, these enzymes protect cell walls from 'free radicals', which set off or speed up ageing processes. If these enzymes aren't present or their activity decreases, the ageing process accelerates. The dieting monkeys, in contrast, had youthful levels of 'age-preventing enzymes' and of all the other blood values tested.

CAUTION: Radicals

The metabolic processes, set in motion by the digestion of food, produce so-called free radicals. These are aggressive little bodies that attack cells; they destroy cell walls and can even cause damage to the cell nucleus. Free radicals accelerate the ageing process and promote numerous illnesses like cancer, heart attack, stroke, and cataracts.

Antioxidants can render free radicals harmless. Among these antioxidants are the vitamins A, C, and E, and the trace elements selenium and zinc. Secondary vegetable matter – that is, materials that aren't vitamins and occur only in plant-based foods – also have antioxidative effects. In particular, black and green tea; carrot, tomato, and grape juice; and red wine all contain large amounts of this vegetable matter.

In Biosphere 2, rations were short

There are numerous indications that a reduction in calories can lengthen humans' lifespans as well as animals'. The Biosphere 2 experiment provided important data to support this. In the 1980s, 40 miles north of Arizona, a $150 million 'greenhouse' was built. In this closed-off world, inhabitants – scientists from various fields – were to test the functionality of an artificial ecosystem. The food for all the participants was to be drawn from things produced within the green-house. On 26 September 1991, four men and four women between the ages of 25 and 67 moved into the giant steel-and-glass container in the Arizona desert. Among them was the well-known American age researcher Roy Walford. The biosphere contained such varying ecosystems as rainforest, savannah, farmland, and desert. But after a short amount of time it became clear that the food these areas produced was not as plentiful as expected, and the inhabitants had to get by with relatively little food over a longer period of time. They took in about 1,800 calories a day. Their diets were mostly vege-tarian; there was meat only once a week, and rarely milk or eggs. In order to avoid vitamin deficiencies, the biosphere inhabitants received daily supplements of vitamins A, B-12, C, and E as well as folic acid. In light of numerous laboratory tests, Walford determined that within a short amount of time, the participants' cholesterol and blood sugar levels – both risk factors for premature ageing and arteriosclerosis – had dropped significantly as a result of the calorie reduction. Changes in the immune system were also noticeable. The functioning of the lymph cells (lymphocytes) and of the neutrophils – both important antibodies – could be improved through the calorie reduction.[18] This is clear proof that antibodies can be strengthened by fasting. Today, Walford stays fit with a 1,500-calorie 'youthfulness diet', and he feels 'mentally alert like never before, full of energy and *joie de vivre*'. Walford is of the view that eating only 1,500 calories a day, along with sufficient amounts of vitamins, minerals, and amino acids, can help us live to be about 120 and at the same time keep us productive and youthful for longer.

Walford's theory is confirmed by healthy and fit centenarians who were interviewed about their lifestyle. In a study of the eating habits of 217 100-year-olds conducted by Franke, interviewees said they had been 'bad eaters' their whole lives.[19] The average caloric intake of these elderly people lay between 1,200 and 1,900 calories a day, so Walford's low-calorie diet is right in the middle. It's worth noting that very old, healthy people are generally underweight and have been thin all their lives.

Less fuel for the furnace

There are countless theories as to why fasting days or calorie reduction have a rejuvenating effect. One reason could be the effect on body temperature. Most people get cold faster when they're eating less or fasting occasionally. The reason for this is a slight lowering of body temperature. This is normally about 37°C (98.6°F). This temperature is maintained by metabolic processes that produce heat. If we eat less, the body's 'furnace' has less 'fuel' to use, and body temperature can sink by 0.3–0.5°C (0.5–0.9°F). This drop in temperature, though slight, causes several processes within the body to happen more slowly – including those that help the ageing process – and saves life energy. This is most likely one of the mechanisms that helps fasting lengthen your life.

Does less food make you more intelligent?

Mice that had been put on diets learned more easily even when they aged. The lean fare prevented age-related loss of co-ordination and improved their ability to learn.

The control group had much worse results in these tests. In addition, the underfed mice performed better in exercise tests on a hamster wheel – they were simply more willing to move than were their well-fed contemporaries.

How fasting delays the ageing process and lengthens life

'A fool is one who does not know that a little is more than a lot. Praise be the spare meal and the moderate drink.' This was the recommendation of the Greek poet Hesiod (c. 800 BC). In order to make your introduction to our fasting programme pleasant for you, we'd like to remind you once again of the countless benefits and rejuvenating effects of the programme. A reduction of calorie intake cures several common health problems. For example, within a short amount of time, blood pressure is lowered. In many cases, blood pressure medications can be reduced or even eliminated. (You should, of course, discuss this with your doctor!) Just as quickly, you will notice a lowering of your blood sugar level. This means a reduced risk for diabetes. Blood cholesterol levels, too, will in most cases become normal. In the long term, there's significantly less risk of arteriosclerosis and circulatory disease.

During the fasting phases, the age-dependent change in activity of many genes is positively affected. These genes control various body functions and metabolic processes. If genes become more active by fasting, the entire organism's functionality will increase.

When we eat less, our body temperature drops. As a result, metabolism slows down and energy use decreases.

The immune system also improves during short periods of fasting; antibodies grow stronger and are more effective against infections and cancerous cells.

Metabolism – programmed for fasting

Metabolism, and therefore also calorie use, is neither constant throughout your lifetime nor the same in everyone. The metabolism can use up more or fewer calories and thereby more or less life energy depending on nutrition and life situation. Our bodies are ruled by the principle of supply and demand. If we take in a large number of calories every day, the metabolism's requirements gradually increase, and it burns more energy. In addition, metabolism is accelerated by smoking, sports, and physical activity.

On the other hand, energy use goes into conservation mode when the body receives fewer calories over a long period of time. This energy-saving mechanism has caused many dieters to despair. After a few weeks of dieting, the pounds refuse to keep dropping, because the body has become accustomed to working with the new, reduced number of calories. But this 'energy-saving metabolism programme' has also ensured the survival of humanity during times of hunger. Because of it, human beings were able to survive periods of short rations. After a few weeks of this, their bodies, too, pulled the 'emergency brake' and so were able to survive bad times on sometimes less than 1,000 calories a day.

The turning on of the 'energy-saving metabolism programme' also protects our energy reserves in the long run, which is why calorie reduction can be used to lengthen our lives. A reduction in nutrient intake, or even the use of regular fasting breaks, seems to be an effective way to live longer. In addition to a conservation of life energy, fewer free radicals develop as a result of a decelerated metabolism. Because of this, the ageing process is slowed. The immune system improves and is better able to defend the body from illness. Risk factors like high blood pressure, high cholesterol levels, and high blood sugar levels are normalised. Your body temperature drops when fasting, which slows the metabolism even more.

Calorie reduction improves the immune system[20]

Just as with human beings, the immune system of ageing mice grows weaker. In particular, the antibodies that are directed against viruses and cancerous cells begin to fail. Studies have shown that the antibodies in a group of ageing mice were stronger when they had less to eat. A calorie reduction was able to:

★ prevent tumours or delay their start
★ strengthen antibodies against viruses
★ boost the production of antibodies
★ improve the number and effectiveness of antibodies (T-lymphocytes)

Does fasting prevent cancer?

Even regularly undertaken low-calorie diet days can benefit your health. It's possible that even a few days of fasting a year can reduce the risk of cancer, and even reduce the number of cancerous cells. A research team in Vienna at the Institute for Tumour Biology and Cancer Research was able to support this conclusion, at least in studies of animals. Schulte-Hermann and his colleagues had one group of rats that fasted for eight days straight, while another group received 60% fewer calories than usual over a course of three months. They examined the liver tissue, which dies off at a regular rate due to normal cell death. What they noticed was that, during fasting, most of the cells that died off were the ones in the process of becoming cancerous.[21]

Getting the right amount of calories

Maybe you've grown curious and would like to experience the benefits of calorie reduction for yourself. The following are different ways to reduce your total number of calories:

★ eating smaller portions at every meal
★ skipping breakfast ('breakfast cancelling')
★ skipping dinner ('dinner cancelling')
★ one day of fasting a week
★ three days of fasting a month
★ one week of fasting three times a year

Which you choose depends largely on your personal preference. The only important thing is that you regularly eat less and do so for the long term. You should make certain you're not adding the saved calories back in through other meals.

If you decide to eat less overall – although this method is the hardest for people to follow – you must first determine your individual calorie amount. This depends on your body size, weight, and workload. Scientists who research the positive effects of calorie reduction recommend a daily energy intake between 1,500 and 2,200 calories. Your daily energy amount should also be within this range. The important thing, though, is that your weight (dependent on your height) shouldn't be below that given in our table of appropriate weights (see Appendix 2: The proper weight for adults). If you're underweight, you should gradually increase your daily calorie amount.

PLEASE NOTE!

Our recommendations for calorie intake and fasting are intended exclusively for healthy adults. They aren't meant for children, adolescents, pregnant women, or breast-feeding mothers, all of whom require more calories. Our suggestions are also not appropriate for people with eating disorders such as anorexia or bulimia. People who suffer from any other disease should first obtain their doctor's permission.

If you only eat a little, the proportions have to be right

You don't have to be a nutrition expert to feed yourself correctly. However, with a reduced calorie intake the composition of your diet is much more important, since you need to be careful to avoid nutrient deficiencies. The following tips and rules of thumb should help keep you from feeling hungry even with a reduced calorie intake and help optimise your intake of vital nutrients:

★ Make sure you have the right proportions of the basic food groups.
★ Follow a 3:1 ratio of carbohydrates to proteins.
★ Eat half raw, half cooked foods.
★ It's better to eat complex carbohydrates than simple ones.
★ Choose low-fat rather than high-fat foods.
★ Supplement water-soluble vitamins and minerals (**Note:** Supplements of vitamins A, D, and E aren't advised during fasting because they require fat in order to be absorbed properly by the body).

The right balance of food groups

About 50–55% of your calorie intake should consist of carbohydrates such as fruit, vegetables, bread and other grains, rice, pasta, and potatoes.

A maximum of 20–25% of your calories should be consumed in the form of fat. Pay attention to the hidden fats in meat, cheese, eggs, chocolate, and cake.

You should eat about 0.015 oz of protein per pound of body weight (1 gram per kilogram). Protein is found above all in fish, meat, dairy, and legumes such as soya products.

You will be following this distribution of the food groups if you put together your diet – with an intake of 1,700 calories – according to the following guidelines:

Daily:
★ six servings (100 cal. each) of fruit or vegetables
★ five servings (100 cal. each) of grains
★ four servings (100 cal. each) of dairy
★ two servings (100 cal. each) of fish, meat, game, or poultry

The lists below and over the page contain suggestions for 100-calorie portions from each food group:

SERVINGS OF FOOD THAT CONTAIN 100 CALORIES EACH (ALL MEASUREMENTS ARE APPROXIMATE)			
FRUITS/VEGETABLES			
apples	200 g	kiwi fruit	200 g
asparagus (cooked)	1500 g	lettuce	1000 g
bananas	120 g	chinese cabbage	1000 g
bell peppers	500 g	oranges	200 g
broccoli	400 g	pears	200 g
carrots	400 g	peas	150 g
cauliflower	400 g	pineapple	200 g
cherries	180 g	strawberries	300 g
corn	90 g	tomatoes	500 g
cucumbers	800 g	watermelon	400 g
aubergines	500 g	courgettes	500 g
green beans	300 g		

DAIRY PRODUCTS

buttermilk	300 ml	milk (3.5% fat)	200 ml
camembert (60% fat)	25 g	milk (skimmed)	300 ml
camembert (30% fat)	50 g	yogurt (3.5% fat)	180 g
cottage cheese	100 g	yogurt (skimmed)	300 g
gouda	25 g		

FISH, MEAT, POULTRY, GAME

beef (lean)	100 g	pork (lean)	100 g
chicken	100 g	prawns	100 g
cod	150 g	salmon	100 g
halibut	100 g	white sea bass	120 g
mackerel	100 g	turkey	100 g

WHOLE GRAINS, SIDE DISHES

bread	50 g	potatoes	150 g
cornflakes	30 g	rice	30 g (uncooked)
pasta	30 g (uncooked)	rolled oats	30 g

The 3:1 Principle of carbohydrates and proteins

In order to avoid feeling hungry and to eat a balanced diet, it's important to eat carbohydrates (potatoes, pasta, rice, bread) and proteins (meat, fish, eggs, legumes, dairy products, tofu) in the right proportions. Carbohydrates deliver important minerals and – because of their high fibre content – leave you feeling satisfied for a long time. In addition, they generally contain fewer calories than protein-rich foods like meat. This is why a meal should consist of three parts carbohydrates and one part protein, at most. The portion of carbohydrate-rich foods should be three times as large as that of the protein-rich foods, to give a simple rule. If this principle is followed at all meals, most people will take in fewer calories than usual. If you aren't as hungry as usual, the portions should be reduced accordingly so that the proportions remain correct.

Half raw + half cooked = well nourished

But how do vitamins fit into a reduced-calorie diet? We recommend that you take in a large part of your calories in the form of vegetable products, since this is where essential nutrients are concentrated; that is, the proportions of vitamins, minerals, and trace elements, and calories are well balanced. In addition, research has shown that organic produce consistently contains higher levels of vitamin C, iron, magnesium, and phosphorus than produce grown with conventional fertilisers or farming systems.[22] Therefore, the more organic produce eaten, the better.

Someone who eats at least six servings every day of as many different fruits and vegetables as possible can be relatively certain that he or she is getting most of the essential vitamins and minerals – providing the produce is fairly fresh. In the winter, or with fruits and vegetables that have been stored for long periods of time, this isn't always the case. Pay close attention to the quality of your food. If the vegetables are crisp and the lettuce hasn't lost its springiness, then – in most cases – relatively few nutrients have been lost. If the leaves are limp and tired, though, or the vegetables are overcooked and the lettuce has brown edges, then the nutrients are no longer sufficient. Since some vitamins are lost quickly after a fruit or vegetable has been sliced due to contact with the air, dishes should be prepared as freshly as possible. It doesn't always have to be six servings of raw fruits and vegetables, though. If you want to feed yourself as well as possible, you should live by the motto 'half raw, half cooked'. Some nutrients can be digested much better in cooked foods. We can process only about 10% of the beta-carotene, an element of vitamin A, in raw carrots, since the raw vegetable's cell walls are so thick that the nutrients can't be absorbed completely. In cooked carrots, however, we can digest the carotene fully. It's similar with tomatoes, so no one should have a guilty conscience about loving spaghetti with tomato sauce or keeping the ketchup bottle within easy reach. Lycopene, a hormone similar to a vitamin, can be absorbed much better from cooked tomatoes than raw ones.

Complex carbohydrates last longer

Your side dishes should consist for the most part of the so-called complex carbohydrates. Complex carbohydrates are mainly found in wholegrain bread, legumes, potatoes, fruit, and vegetables. From these foods, sugar makes its way slowly into the blood and blood sugar levels rise only very slowly – this keeps you from getting tired right after lunch and keeps you full for a long time. The longer the sugar takes to get into the bloodstream, the longer you will feel satisfied – an important aspect of a reduced-calorie diet.

An ideal side dish for energy-conscious people is pasta, often unfairly described as fattening. Pasta made of durum wheat flour contains what is called a resistant starch. The processing and drying of the pasta causes the carbohydrates to change so drastically that they can't be fully processed by our bodies. Because of this, some of the 'noodle calories' don't even enter into the equation. Caution is more advisable with regard to pasta sauces, which generally contain a lot of calories.

Supplementing vital nutrients

In a reduced-calorie diet, you must pay careful attention to the composition of your foods. Produce and fish, in particular, provide important nutrients that can protect us from the ageing process. Foods that will give you valuable nutrients in a low-calorie diet are, for example, citrus fruits and currants (vitamin C), apricots and carrots (vitamin A, beta carotene), peanuts, almonds, wheat germ, and cold-pressed oils (vitamin E, folic acid, vitamin B-6), fish, lean meat, and grain products (selenium, zinc, vitamin B-6, and B-12). Also, keep in mind that organic produce is preferable because it contains dramatically lower levels of toxins and pollutants.

Even so, it's not always guaranteed that the products we buy at the supermarket still contain all their vital nutrients. There are different reasons for this:

★ We buy fruit and vegetables that have been stored for a long time. After being harvested, fruit loses vitamins daily.

★ We cook most foods before eating them. It's well known that heat destroys important vitamins.

★ High air-pollution levels, bad nutrition, exercise, and stress are just a few of the situations that overload us and increase our need for certain vitamins (antioxidants).

★ Particularly if our calorie intake is reduced because of fasting, it can become necessary to supplement our everyday diet with vitamins, minerals, and trace elements.

WE RECOMMEND THE FOLLOWING COMBINATION OF DAILY SUPPLEMENTS	
vitamin A	once a day: 5000 IU (approx. 1500 mcg) with a meal (pregnant women shouldn't take vitamin A)
vitamin C	twice a day: 250 mg
vitamin E	once a day: 400 IU (approx. 268 mg) with a meal
folic acid	once a day: 600 mcg
vitamin B-1 (Thiamin)	once a day: 5 mg
vitamin B-2 (Riboflavin)	once a day: 5 mg
vitamin B-3 (Niacin)	twice a day: 25 mg
vitamin B-6	once a day: 10 mg
vitamin B-12	once a day:100 mcg
selenium	once a day: 50 mcg
zinc	once a day: 12–15 mg
magnesium	once a day: 400 mg before bedtime
calcium	twice a day: 500 mg
IU = International Unit, mcg = microgram, mg = milligram.	

Further recommendations for supplementing essential nutrients in special situations can be found in Appendix 3: Our vitamin recommendations for special situations.

How to get rid of your fat

There are different ways to save calories as well as energy. Probably the easiest solution for most is to trade some very high-fat foods for similar low-fat products. Fat is more than plentiful in most British people's diets, with many of us taking in over 30% of our daily calories in fat. The results are obesity and health problems. Asians, who are generally slim, eat differently. They take in only 15% of their daily diet in the form of fat, while carbohydrates and proteins play a starring role in traditional Japanese and Chinese meals.

Often there's more fat in a single meal than we should eat in a day. A fast-food hamburger, such as a Big Mac, with a medium fries contains about 49 grams of fat; a croissant contains about 15; and even half a cup of roasted peanuts has 24. Just look at our examples for high-fat and low-fat breakfasts as well as the overview of high-fat and low-fat alternatives that follows the recipes. You'll be amazed by how easy it is to save calories.

High-fat breakfast:
★ 2 croissants, 20 g butter (about 1½ tbsp)
★ 1 egg
★ 2 tbsp chocolate hazelnut spread
★ A cup of cocoa

Fat content: 91 grams

Low-fat breakfast:
★ 2 wholegrain rolls
★ 20 g margarine (about 1½ tbsp)
★ 2 slices of low-fat cheese with 20% fat
★ 2 tsp honey
★ A cup of tea

Fat content: 10 grams

Since 1 gram of fat contains 9 calories, you're saving 81 grams of fat with the low-fat breakfast, or 729 calories from fat.

Fatty foods in particular provide large numbers of calories. In the context of a reduced-calorie diet, you should replace high-fat foods with low-fat products. The table below lists some suggestions for foods that can be substituted for foods higher in fat so as to make your meals more healthy.

HIGH-FAT FOODS AND LOW-FAT ALTERNATIVES

HIGH-FAT FOODS		LOW-FAT FOODS, THE BETTER ALTERNATIVE	
croissant	25 g fat	wholegrain roll	<1 g fat
1 tsp (20 g) hazelnut-chocolate spread	6 g fat	1 tsp (20 g) honey	0 g fat
1 tsp (20 g) peanut butter	10 g fat	1 tsp (20 g) marmalade	0 g fat
1 cup (150 ml) cocoa	2 g fat	1 cup (150 ml) tea	0 g fat
1 cup (200 ml) coffee with milk	2 g fat	1 cup (150 ml) black coffee	0 g fat
1 danish pastry with nuts (150 g)	40 g fat	1 piece of brioche (150 g)	4 g fat
1 scoop ice cream	14 g fat	1 scoop of sorbet	1 g fat
1 glass (200 ml) cow's milk, 3.5% fat	7 g fat	1 glass cow's milk, 0.3% fat or 1 glass buttermilk	<1 g fat 1 g fat
1 yogurt (150 g), 3.5% fat	6 g fat	1 yogurt (150 g), 0.3% fat	<1 g fat
chocolate pudding (125 g)	4 g fat	gelatin dessert	0 g fat
1 slice cheese (20 g), 45% fat	6 g fat	1 slice cheese (20 g), 20% fat	2 g fat
hamburger (75% lean)	28 g fat	roast beef (150 g) or turkey steak (150 g)	6 g fat 2 g fat
egg yolk	6 g fat	egg white	<1 g fat
tuna fish (150 g)	23 g fat	squid	1 g fat
salmon (150 g)	20 g fat	white sea bass	1 g fat

Heart attack after a big feast[23]
Heart attacks can be brought on by overeating. Doctors from the Brigham and Women's Hospital in Boston interviewed 2000 heart attack patients. Of these, 158 claimed to have eaten much more than usual the day before the attack.

Five meals a day will speed up the ageing process

If you want to take in fewer calories in the long term in order to conserve life energy, you must shift your metabolism into a lower gear. To do so, you can, of course, simply reduce your daily calorie count by eating less at each meal. But in our experience this isn't easy for most people. In addition, it's difficult to judge the number of calories you actually eat. Even the American age researcher Roy Walford, who researched the rejuvenating effect of fasting, admits that he can't always stick to a daily 'fasting programme' or a constant diet in which you eat half as much as usual.[24] It's usually easier to reduce the total number of calories by skipping individual meals.

Until now it has always been recommended that you eat five small meals a day. This way of eating is thought to keep hunger at bay, making you thin and healthy. This is probably not quite true, except for patients who suffer from diabetes or other chronic illnesses. Frequent mealtimes prevent the release of the rejuvenating growth hormone somatotropin (STH). Fasting, or skipping meals, on the other hand, is good for our hormone system; the blood sugar level – and consequently the level of insulin, which lowers blood sugar – decreases only when the stomach is empty for a longer period of time. Insulin, which is released from the pancreas whenever we eat, prevents the release of growth hormones. Having an empty stomach and a low insulin level, in contrast, induces the body to release STH from the pituitary gland. These growth hormones are really like a jack-of-all-trades for our bodies when it comes to their rejuvenating effect. In 1990 an American, Dr Rudman, was able to prove that, under the influence of the growth hormone, the following changes take place:

★ muscle mass increases
★ fat deposits are reduced
★ the immune system is strengthened
★ the skin grows tauter
★ bone density increases[25]

By skipping single meals, you aren't just saving energy, you're lengthening the phases where your stomach is empty and improving your growth hormone output. The best rejuvenating effect can be reached by skipping dinner ('dinner cancelling') or breakfast ('breakfast cancelling'). An alternative option is to take occasional fasting days.

Larks eat breakfast, owls eat at night

Whether it's better for you to skip the morning or the evening meal depends on whether you have the biorhythm of a lark or an owl. People who like to sleep late and have trouble getting going in the morning are usually less hungry in the morning. It's usually easier for them to skip breakfast. These 'night owls' only really become active at night. Therefore, they place more value on dinner and would do better to cancel breakfast.

It's completely different for 'larks'; lark people are morning people who jump out of bed full of energy. For them, breakfast is simply part of starting the day out right, while dinner is often easier to skip. Whichever possibility you choose depends entirely on your personal preference.

Another possible way to save energy and simultaneously raise your growth hormone level is to take fasting days. Depending on your personal preference, you can take one fasting day a week or three consecutive days a month.

Cancelling breakfast

'Owls' in particular find it relatively easy to give up breakfast, so breakfast cancelling is ideal for them. It is, however, important that you drink plenty of fluids. You should drink about one litre of tea, mineral water, or malt coffee every morning. A *café au lait* or a glass of juice can make the start of your day easier, too. If you want to ease yourself into breakfast cancelling, you can start by eating a fruit breakfast. This means eating up to 300 grams of fruit over the course of the morning, particularly apples, pears, strawberries, peaches, or kiwis. The advantage of the fruit breakfast is that fruit is fat-free and does not provide any hard-to-digest calories; your calorie intake is much lower than a normal breakfast, but your stomach isn't empty.

Cancelling dinner

Another way to conserve energy is to give up dinner. 'Leave dinner to your enemies', says an old Chinese proverb. Maybe even in those days people knew of the many healthy effects of skipping the evening meal.

Dinner cancelling is best suited for 'larks'. This successful method of lengthening one's life has been practised by, among others, Cardinal König, the former Viennese Archbishop, who died recently aged 98 (1905–2004). He reported that he had been practising dinner cancelling since the age of 50. The Cardinal reduced his dinner to a roasted apple with a little honey, which he ate between 7:00 and 8:00 pm. This 'dinner' contained just enough sugar molecules to keep hunger from disturbing his sleep. His actual dinner was 'cancelled – erased without a substitute'.[26] It's important that you don't eat twice as much breakfast the next morning, because this would negate the effects of skipping dinner.

One day of fasting a week? No problem!

For most people it's very hard to lower daily calorie intake. It's easier, on the other hand, to eat normally during the week and fast one day during the weekend. This, too, will reduce the total number of calories eaten per week. Walford, the American researcher, lives by this principle and feels good about it.[27] Because of the one fasting day, he can eat normally during the week and still save calories. You can't, of course, eat the extra calories the day after fasting. If you live by this rule for a year, you'll have saved 104,000 to 156,000 calories. This is equal to fasting for seven-and-a-half weeks at a time.

Occasional fasting days are inconsequential for healthy people, and are common in almost all religions. During the year, the Catholic church has multiple fasting days and days of abstinence. Muslims eat nothing in the daytime during Ramadan, which lasts for a month. For Jews and Buddhists, too, fasting plays an important role – Jews traditionally fast on Yom Kippur, and Buddhists commonly practise fasting as a form of self-discipline, especially on full moon days.[28] Unfortunately, few people still hold themselves to these rules. The religious significance of these days may have lost importance for many people, and they haven't yet recognised the advantages of fasting for their health.

Anyone can fast

Anyone who is healthy can fast for one day or one week. It's not hard for our bodies to get by for a short time without food. Regular fasting can lower total calorie intake. Our bodies are, in fact, programmed for regular fasting; before the invention of the refrigerator and the pantry, there were often periods in which food was scarce. Unlike with a reduced-calorie diet, where most people's stomachs growl all the time, with fasting the feeling of hunger disappears after one or two days. In addition to weight loss, which is the first noticeable result for most fasters, energy use is lowered in the long run, the metabolism slows down, the ageing process is held back, and life energy is saved. If you decide to fast, you will notice other positive changes as well. Especially worth noting here is that fasting relieves strain on the circulatory system, cleanses the body, and activates the immune system. The mental aspect shouldn't be disregarded, either. When fasting, the body is more ready to relax; during this time, autogenic training or other relaxation techniques are easiest to learn. Your stress level sinks. Fasting gives the concepts of denial and enjoyment a new meaning, and your self-awareness will profit from your achievement.

If you decide on a fasting period of several days, follow the suggestions below:

★ Choose the right time period. Extremely stressful professional or personal times aren't ideal. Fasting is also inappropriate at times of acute illness; in cases of chronic illness, consult your doctor first.
★ Don't eat solid foods.
★ Drink at least two, if possible three, litres of water, tea, vegetable broth, or juice. Drink more than you think you need.
★ Promote excretion. If you normally visit a sauna, continue doing so. Exercise in moderation is also allowed, but do not overexert yourself. We recommend peripatetic meditation (see pages 37–38).
★ Wear warmer clothes. Most people get cold when they fast.

Fasting – renewal for the body
Longer periods of fasting have far-reaching effects on the entire organism.

Brain
Your brain slows down to conserve energy when fasting, too. Observation skills and concentration are reduced, although some fasters say that they're more creative during this time.

Eyes
During fasting, it becomes more difficult to focus your eyes, particularly on print. The reason for this is a lower pressure in the eyes. Be careful when driving! After fasting, your eyesight will return to normal; some even claim to see better than before.

Digestive organs

Your 'growling' stomach will be quiet after one or, at most, two days. Your feeling of hunger will disappear because your body is now feeding off its reserves. This is why fasting is usually easier than just 'eating less'.

Circulatory system

Your blood pressure is lower, so don't jump out of bed too fast in the morning. It's better to shower right after getting up to prepare your body for mild movement.

Urine

Your urine can become temporarily darker and potent. It's important to drink more fluids than your thirst seems to require.

Skin

During fasting, your skin will be drier; your sweat will smell strong and unpleasant. Shower more often and use a good moisturiser. After fasting, your skin will be significantly smoother and softer.

Mouth

Your tongue may be coated more heavily; the coating is sometimes dark yellow or brown. Your mouth will taste stale, and you may have bad breath. Brush your teeth several times a day, use more mouth-wash than usual, and chew on a lemon rind. This stimulates saliva production and eliminates bad breath.

Weight

A common reason to start a fasting regimen is to lose weight. At the beginning, pounds will seem to melt away. This initial weight loss, however, is mostly water and salt. Do not be disappointed when your weight loss does not continue at the same pace after a few days. In order to lose a pound of fat tissue, you must save between 6,000 and 7,000 calories, that is, at least three or four days of fasting. Since the metabolism begins to run more slowly during a fast, it's in energy-saving mode and using fewer calories, so most people gain the weight back quickly after a 'starvation diet' when they resume normal eating habits.

Metabolism

The body is switching from a synthesising, anabolic metabolism to a disintegrative, catabolic metabolic state. Fat tissue is dismantled (lipolysis), but a certain amount of protein, too, which is stored mostly in the muscles, is lost. Moderate exercise can help prevent you from losing muscle mass. Ketone bodies – for example, acetic acid and hydroxybutyrate – are a by-product of the loss of these 'fat pockets'. The acetone odour of these metabolic by-products contributes to the pungent smell of a fasting person. Ketone bodies can be found in urine.

CAUTION: Gout can make fasting painful

One thing requires particular caution: uric acid increases during fasting. People who have a tendency towards gout need to be especially careful. The cause of this is the increase in cell disintegration. If uric acid levels rise over 6.5 to 7.0 mg/dl, a painful attack of gout could be the result. If you tend to have high uric acid levels, you should drink at least 2.5, preferably 3 litres of water or juice a day. In addition, you should be taking medication to treat your uric acid levels. After a week of fasting, the levels will gradually become lower again.

A few more words about stimulants

Caffeine uses up calories

The most common stimulant is unquestionably coffee. It's especially valued for the stimulant effect of the caffeine it contains. Each cup contains 70 to 150 mg of caffeine; but few coffee drinkers can get by on one cup a day, since the stimulating effect fades away almost as quickly as it sets in. About 30 minutes after enjoying a cup of coffee, the caffeine has already had its maximum effect; after three to six hours, half of it has already been processed and has disappeared. In smokers, the effect goes away much more quickly; this may be why most heavy smokers are also excessive coffee drinkers.

But caffeine does not just make you alert; it also stimulates your metabolism, increasing your calorie use. This metabolism-stimulating effect is also known as a 'thermogenic effect'. The thermogenesis initiated by caffeine stimulates the dismantling of fat in the body (lipolysis). Extra energy is released from the body's reserves.

Non-smokers save energy

Almost every smoker has an excuse at the ready for why he or she can't quit smoking: I'll get fat. Most ex-smokers do, in fact, gain weight. A large study examined the well-known phenomenon of weight gain and increased appetite in former smokers. A study of 5,000 people showed that ten years after giving up cigarettes, ex-smokers were significantly heavier than their counterparts who never smoked. In men this meant a weight gain of 9.7 lbs (4.4 kg), and in women, about 11 lbs (5 kg).[29] For most smokers, the unwanted weight gain is a major reason to keep puffing. But why do they gain weight? The reason for this is that their metabolism had been sped up dramatically by the contents of cigarettes. Every cigarette increases calorie use and contributes to the wasting of life energy. The weight gain is a sign that your metabolism is finally calming down after quitting smoking and is shifting gears again. According to our theory, this is actually a good sign. If you take our tips to heart after quitting smoking, you won't need to worry about the extra pounds.

Summary

★ The only method proven to lengthen life and slow the ageing process in mammals, including humans, is a reduction in energy use and a slowing of the metabolism by restricting calorie intake.

★ Calorie reduction isn't recommended for children, growing adolescents, or pregnant women. It's also not intended for people with anorexia or bulimia. People with other illnesses should consult their doctors first.

★ When reducing calorie intake, it's important to pay attention to the composition of your meals. Supplementing your diet with vitamins, minerals, and trace elements should be a part of this.

★ You can reduce calorie intake by restricting the amount eaten at each meal, by skipping meals (breakfast or dinner), or by fasting occasionally.

Chapter Four

Laziness is at the heart of good health

4

'Sometimes I sits and thinks; and sometimes I just sits.'
— Satchel Paige (1906–1982), American baseball player

This chapter covers:
- ★ **how to save energy by being patient**
- ★ **why wounds heal better when you're on holiday**
- ★ **why relaxing makes you smarter**
- ★ **why being lazy strengthens your immune system**
- ★ **the importance of indolence for your health**
- ★ **how you can avoid tension and stress**

Stress costs you energy

Not only physical labour, but also mental labour costs you strength and energy, particularly if it's performed under stressful conditions.

The body's metabolism is constantly controlled by hormones. Calorie use changes depending on which hormones are released.

It's well known that the stress hormones adrenaline and noradrenaline speed up metabolism, increasing calorie use by 10 to 15%. Assuming that we use up about 2,000 calories without stress and with low physical exertion, under stress we burn an extra 200 to 300 calories of life energy per day.

Stress: life-saving for prehistoric humans – harmful for civilised humans

Stress isn't a twentieth-century phenomenon. It's as old as humanity. In murky prehistoric times, enemy tribes, hunger, and wild animals were the main stress factors, and today lack of time, deadlines, bureaucracy, waiting in line, ill-tempered superiors, and managing our work/life balance drive our pulse and blood pressure to new levels and rob us of energy.

Even after thousands of years, the human body in today's civilised world reacts to stress the same way it did for the Neanderthals. When the cerebrum senses a threatening situation, a million-year-old chain reaction instantly occurs in our bodies. The adrenal glands release the stress hormones adrenaline, noradrenaline, and cortisol. These instantly set off several 'emergency programmes' in the body.

Heart rate and blood pressure increase. In acute stress situations – because of the increased levels of stress hormones in the blood – heart rate can increase from 60 to 130 beats per minute in a matter of seconds. Under constant stress, the resting pulse, which is normally around 60 or 70 beats, is increased to 80–90 bpm. This is why someone who is stressed can rarely sit still for any length of time. Stressed people are more hectic, fidget more, and pace nervously around the room. This behaviour, which is an attempt to control your inner unrest, also uses up a lot of life energy. After all, the muscles that are automatically tightened by stress use more calories too.

When the extra hormones released into our bloodstream by the adrenal glands aren't used up, or the stressful situation persists, our bodies become susceptible to illness, both mental and physical. In the long term, a lack of calmness and too few recovery periods lead to a premature wearing out of many organs.

When you're stressed out, you trip yourself up

Stress factors and a lack of relaxation and even-temperedness can have negative physical, mental, and even professional effects. These can include:

Physical effects

★ Stress uses up your life energy prematurely.
The result: your body ages faster and is more susceptible to illnesses.
★ Under stress, your blood pressure rises.
The result: the risk of circulatory disease, heart attack, and stroke increases.
★ Too little relaxation raises stress-hormone levels in your blood.
The result: your immune system is weakened.

Mental effects

★ In stress situations, the cortisol level rises.
The result: your memory grows worse.
★ If you have no time to relax, certain parts of the brain can be damaged in the long term.
The result: your brain ages faster.

Professional effects

★ A lack of even-temperedness makes you tense.
The result: you won't be trusted with a leadership position.
★ You make more mistakes in stress situations.
The result: you're bad for business.
★ Your lack of even-temperedness makes for a bad work environment.
The result: your colleagues and co-workers are less motivated.

Even-temperedness and laziness – your body's balanced programme

Relaxation, even-temperedness, and even occasional laziness and indolence are your body's way of balancing itself out. This is in order to conserve your strength and energy reserves, and to save life energy.

During these times, the body switches from the so-called

sympathetic nervous system, which makes our bodies run on high, to the calming parasympathetic nervous system. Your pulse and breathing are normalised, you take deeper breaths, your blood pressure is regulated.

Your energy use decreases. Your immune system, which under stress is weakened by the constant high level of cortisol, recovers. Thought processes can once again occur without being hindered, and stress-related 'blackouts' suddenly cease.

But rest and relaxation don't happen automatically. Worries, fears, and work-related problems aren't that easy to shake off. Because of this, relaxation must often be initiated consciously and integrated into your daily schedule.

Although stress was not unknown to our ancestors, periods of relaxation and meditation used to be planned into their daily or yearly routines. In the winter months, work slowed; on weekends, religious services could create a distance from everyday life; and periods of fasting were a time for contemplation. These islands of relaxation, phases of inactivity, and times of indolence are missing from life today. Deadline pressure and competitive thinking seem to leave no room for meditation and contemplation. In order to stay healthy despite stress, it's important for us to keep a balance between tension and relaxation. Only if you make sure to balance out times of stress and leave room in your daily routine for rest and relaxation will you be able to defy stress, conserve your strength, save energy reserves, and increase your chance of a long and healthy life.

Relaxing makes you more intelligent

Who doesn't remember this scene from school days: at home, in a relaxed atmosphere, you could say the poem backwards and forwards, you knew all the vocabulary on the list, and even multiplication didn't present any problems. But as soon as you were put on the spot, standing up in front of the class, your heart pounded like mad and your head was empty. Even though those days are behind you, the fact remains that your brain works better in a relaxed state, making you more productive and quick-witted. Regular periods of relaxation can help prevent a premature breakdown of your grey matter. Constant stress, on the other hand, accelerates the rate at which your brain ages. Humans aren't the only ones whose mental health suffers from stress caused by fear, anger, sadness, and worry. Animals, too, degenerate mentally when they're under stress and have no time for relaxation.

An American team conducting medical research into the way the brain ages, determined that constant stress can damage rats' brain cells. Philip Landfield and his colleagues from the University of Kentucky created stressful conditions for the rats comparable to that of workers who are constantly waiting for the boss's next outburst, and discovered that after just three weeks (five days a week) certain parts of the brain showed signs of change. The hippocampus region was most affected. This part of the brain is an important filter for the senses. This is where unimportant impressions are sorted out, to make sure only vital information gets through to the cerebral cortex. Under stress, this filter doesn't work properly any more; unimportant stimuli flood the brain, concentration decreases, and we miss important things. The hippocampus is apparently damaged by an overdose of the body's own stress hormone, cortisol, which is released in tense situations. If a period of rest and relaxation follows, the cortisol level will sink again, and the brain can recover, sustaining no damage.

With most people, the hippocampus shrinks with age, causing mild memory decline, but this decline is far more rapid in the brains of people suffering from Alzheimer's disease. Further studies showed that the stressed rats had lost twice as many brain cells as their relaxed contemporaries. It's already well known that stress hormones like adrenaline and cortisol play a role in the development of heart attacks and high blood pressure. Possibly, though, there's also a connection between stress and the degeneration of mental capacity.

Wounds heal better when you're on holiday

It's not just that we don't deal as well with pain in stress situations – pre-existing wounds don't heal as well, either. This was the conclusion of a study at Ohio State University. Scientists gave dentistry students small cuts on their gums during the summer holidays, and some years later just before their final exams. During exams, the wounds took 40% longer to heal than during the relaxing summer holiday. Interleukin-1 values, a transmitter in the immune system that plays an important role in healing wounds, were two-thirds lower over the exam period than during holidays.

Happy mothers – healthy children

Humour and a good attitude aren't just important for your own immune system – infants who are breastfed also benefit from their mother's good moods. Swiss immunologists Hodel and Grob reported that contented breast-feeding mothers have raised levels of immunoglobulin A.[30] These antibodies protect against infections in the mucous membrane. What's interesting is that not only the happy mothers, but also their newborns, had fewer infections of the air passages.

Contentment keeps your blood vessels clear

It's possible that even-temperedness and a positive attitude can be good for our blood vessels and protect them from arteriosclerosis. Doctors at Duke University in Durham, North Carolina, discovered that a low level of the neurotransmitter serotonin, often found in people suffering from depression, hastens arteriosclerosis. In contented, relaxed, and even-tempered people, however, serotonin levels are significantly higher and the danger to blood vessels significantly lower.[31]

How high is your stress level?

We've known for a long time, and doctors have noticed again and again, that people are at greater risk from illness after intense periods of stress. A psychiatrist named Thomas H. Holmes from the Department of Medicine at the University of Washington studied the connections between stress and illness and developed a scale that made it possible to evaluate individual stressors.[32] Naturally, not every stressful life situation is represented in this scale. In our opinion, everyday stress factors in particular are dealt with too little. However, the test does give a relatively good overview of common problems in our lives.

The table below shows various events that place stress on us. Some of these situations represent a traumatic event, for example, a divorce. These life occurrences are assigned a much higher stress point value. But even apparently happy events like weddings and births leave their mark on us. The greater the number of stress situations within a short amount of time, and the more energy we must use to overcome them, the more susceptible we become to illness and all kinds of complaints.

Stress test, based on Holmes

WHICH STRESSORS HAVE YOU EXPERIENCED IN THE PAST 12 MONTHS?		
EVENT	TICK	STRESS POINT VALUE
Death of a spouse		100
Divorce		73
Separation		65
Imprisonment		63
Death of a relative		63
Injury or illness		53

Marriage	50
Termination of job	47
Reconciliation with spouse	45
Retirement	45
Illness of a relative	44
Pregnancy	40
Sexual problems	39
New member of family	39
Career change	39
Change in financial situation	38
Death of close friend	37
New job	36
Marital strife	36
Debt	31
More responsibility at work	29
Less responsibility at work	29
Children leave home	29
Difficulties with in-laws	29
Significant personal achievement	28
Spouse goes (back) to work or stops working	26
Starting or finishing school	26
General change in life situation	25
Change in personal habits	24
Problems with boss	24
Change in working hours or conditions	20
Moving	20
Changing schools	20
Change in free-time activities	19
Change in religious or community activity	19
Change in social activity	18
Minor credit problems	17
Change in sleeping habits	16
More family get-togethers than usual	15
Fewer family get-togethers than usual	15
Change in eating habits	15

Holiday	13
Christmas	12
Minor trouble with the law	11
STRESS POINT TOTAL =	

Results from the table

More than 300 stress points in the past 12 months: Look out! 90% of the people who have this many stress points in one year are particularly susceptible to all kinds of illness. You need more energy in order to stay healthy. Our programmes for saving energy and staying calm are especially important for you.

200 to 299 stress points in the past 12 months: You, too, have above-average stress levels. Your risk of getting ill is at about 30%. You should work our suggestions for relaxation and calmness into your everyday routine. Peripatetic meditation (see pages 37–38) can also have a positive effect on your immune system.

100 to 199 stress points in the past 12 months: About one in ten people is particularly prone to illness at this stress level. Your risk is relatively low, but you can still benefit from our energy-saving suggestions.

Less than 100 stress points within the past 12 months: Congratulations! Your stress level is very low.

Eight warning signs of stress

In our hectic everyday lives we often don't notice how much life energy we're wasting because of stress and the pressure to perform. But there are many physical signs that show us we're missing out on rest and relaxation. If you notice two or more of these warning signs, it's time to put the brakes on your stress.

1 **Your neck muscles are tense and sore.** It's for good reason that the trapezius – the muscle that stretches from the back of your neck over your shoulders – is called the 'psycho-muscle'. Numerous studies have shown a connection between emotions and muscle tension. This is why most people experience painful knots in their shoulders and upper back in times of stress.

2 **When your neighbour coughs, you get the flu.** Constant stress harms your immune system. Under stress, an increased amount of cortisol is produced in the adrenal glands. In medical practice, cortisol is used to relax an overactive immune system, for example in the case of an allergy or eczema. But mental overload, too, forces the immune system to work on low power as a result of constant cortisol flow. Typical signs of stress are constant colds, frequent herpes infections, a constant feeling of being out of shape, and susceptibility to every infection that's going around.

3 **Your head is always pounding.** If other diseases have been ruled out, migraines and constant headaches are an unmistakable sign of overload. In addition to the migraine attacks with nausea and drilling pain, there's also often a dull headache that stretches from the nape of your neck to your forehead like a helmet. Anyone who has to take more than two headache pills a month should think about his or her stress level.

4 **You've lost or gained more than 5% of your body weight in the past six months.** Some people lose their appetites because of stress, others can't live without chocolate and cake when they're stressed out. Weight fluctuations cannot be avoided in these situations, and in the long term, productivity and resilience are compromised.

5 **You can't keep your eyes closed at night, and fight sleep during the day.** The body's recovery happens mostly during phases of deep sleep, which repeat about every 90 minutes. Studies of brain waves (ECG) show that these refreshing sleep phases are shortened during times of stress. Despite a sufficient amount of sleep, there's not enough nightly regeneration and recovery. Deep sleep is

interrupted by rapid-eye movement (REM), or dream, phases. This is where the day's events are processed once more in a dream. The day's pressures, stress, and tension can turn into nightmares during REM phases.

6 **Your heartbeat accelerates or skips a beat.** In acute stress situations, heart frequency can go from 60 bpm to 130 bpm or more in a matter of minutes. This is caused by an increase in the stress hormones adrenaline and noradrenaline, which force the heart muscle to work at its highest capacity. Under constant stress, your resting pulse, which is normally at 60 or 70 bpm, is increased to 80 or 90 bpm. In the long term, this leads to a premature wearing out of numerous organs. The unpleasant 'heart skipping' can also be caused by stress, usually in connection with excessive coffee drinking and nicotine consumption. However, make sure that it's not a symptom of heart disease.

7 **You chew over all your problems at night.** Grinding your teeth at night, the 'chewing through' of all your problems in your sleep, occurs almost exclusively in times of stress. Not only may your partner be disturbed by the grinding sounds, but eventually it also leads to a wearing down of your teeth and painful tension in your jaw muscles. If you're not sure whether you're a nocturnal grinder, ask your dentist. He or she can easily identify the signs of wear and tear on your teeth.

8 **Your hands are clammy and cold.** In stress situations, circulation becomes centralised; that is, more blood is sent to important organs like the heart, lungs, and brain, while less blood flows to the hands and feet, which thus feel cold and clammy. A little exercise will get your blood moving again.

Laughter: the number-one stress fighter

Gelotologists – scientists who study laughter – have proven what we've all known for a long time: laughing is healthy. Laughing is pure relief, reduces stress, and makes us calmer. Just one minute of laughter equals 30 minutes of relaxation training. The diaphragm and solar plexus are thoroughly massaged by every peal of laughter, breaths are deeper, tense muscles are relaxed, and the body releases large amounts of its own opiates, which give us energy, make us relaxed, and make it easier to distance ourselves from everyday problems. If you allow yourself to have fun regularly, you're strengthening your immune system and breaking down harmful stress hormones.

At the same time, laughing is an 'internal exercise programme'. Pulse and blood pressure increase slightly, and oxygen intake improves. Sixty seconds of laughing is just as good for our health as ten minutes of running. When your 'laugh training' is over, your pulse and blood pressure sink again. Often they're even lower after the laughing attack than they were before – a good sign that you've reached a more relaxed state by laughing. But we use this inner source of relaxation much too rarely.

Children laugh up to four hundred times a day, while adults laugh fifteen times a day at most – this is bad for our well-being, for our professional and private success. Laughing eliminates the distance between strangers and can even get rid of initial dislikes. It can have a positive effect on your fellow human beings. The highest level of the art of laughing is being able to laugh at yourself, so you should exercise your laugh muscles daily.

In the future, seek out situations that make you laugh. Choose comedies over dramas; train yourself to notice funny things in your daily life; look for absurdity in your surroundings; and above all, learn to laugh at yourself and be more humorous.

Putting stress aside, gaining peace and relaxation

Author Paul Wilson, in his book *Instant Calm*, explains how to get rid of stress and unrest in your life, describing what to do in only two sentences. He writes: 'Either change the circumstances that are placing you under stress, or change the way you deal with them. There aren't many other options.'[33]

We agree with these findings, albeit with a small change. We would delete 'either' and replace the word 'or' with the word 'and'. Only if you use both possibilities can you find your way back to peace and relaxation. At the same time, we recognise that nowadays many of us are subject to professional and personal pressures that can hardly be changed (deadlines, work guidelines, dependence on superiors). On the other hand, we've forgotten how to differentiate important activities from the unimportant. We treat all appointments as if they were equally important. In addition, we multiply our work-related stress by scheduling personal meetings that aren't actually necessary.

It will work just as well without you

In many situations we must let go of something else in order to relax. This is usually what's hardest for us. We're afraid of losing face if we don't follow the goals we initially set, and we think we've failed. We don't want to hurt anyone, and we try to make everyone happy. We think (or hope?) that nothing will work without us – that if we're not there everything will fall apart.

These are false assumptions! Have you never noticed that business goes on as usual when you're ill, on holiday, or have a day off? It will work without you! You don't have to be the captain of your sports team, plan the Christmas party every year, and be a member of the local council if you're under a lot of stress at work or at home.

The first, most important piece of advice we have for you is therefore to refuse extra positions and appointments. Get rid of your ballast in order to find your way back to inner peace and harmony.

Organise tasks by priority

Not all your appointments are equally important. However, many of us make the mistake of assigning all tasks the same importance. We often prefer to do the less important, simpler tasks and accomplish them early, but then in the evening are left with many tasks that absolutely must be done. Establish priorities. Mark all of your appointments, assignments, and errands: red means 'super important', blue means 'needs to be addressed sometime today', and green stands for 'not important, can be postponed'. Take care of all the red-flagged tasks first, starting with the most unpleasant; you'll get to the blue ones later. If there are only green tasks left on your planner in the late afternoon, that's no reason to work overtime – go home!

Get rid of green tasks
Green tasks are so unimportant that you can postpone or even cancel them. Why should you use your valuable energy for something like that? Get rid of the unimportant things that are holding you back. Start by choosing one green task a day that can be eliminated without a replacement. Once you've mastered this exercise, raise the stakes by eliminating two, three, or even more of these green tasks. This will give you extra time to regenerate. Allow yourself a little white lie if there's no other way to get out of a green task.

Advantages of effective stress management:
- ★ Your mental productivity increases.
- ★ Your immune system is strengthened.
- ★ The ageing process slows down.
- ★ The risk of heart attack, high blood pressure, and stroke decreases.
- ★ Migraines decrease.
- ★ You sleep better.

Separate your breaks from your work
Starting immediately, do not combine lunch or dinner with work. Your breaks are yours alone for regeneration and relaxation. Don't read the newspaper while eating, and don't talk about politics, money, or religion at the dinner table. You could end up in an

argument, which robs you of energy. Eat slowly and with pleasure. Eat calmly, and allow yourself a few minutes of contemplation afterwards. Some people like to say a prayer before and after eating, which creates the necessary distance from the outside world.

Make your free time stress-free
When you're stressed at work, the weekend should be used for regeneration and recuperation.

In reality, however, this isn't the case for most of us. If you try to pack as much action, experience, and activity into your free time as possible, you're often only creating more stress for yourself. The wish for harmony and pleasant experiences usually ends in arguments, frustration, and frenzied activity. This is why we're often under just as much pressure in our free time as at work and are exhausted and drained when we return to the office. We advise planning laziness into your free time. Reserve a few hours for indolence and inactivity.

Preventing stress-related gaps in your well-being

You certainly won't succeed immediately in defusing all of these stressful situations. In order to avoid harm during these tension-filled phases, you should make sure you have an adequate intake of protective vital nutrients, because stress increases the need for certain vitamins and minerals. The increased need can't often be filled through your diet alone. In these situations we recommend a temporary daily intake of some of the following vitamins, minerals, and trace elements:

★ **Vitamin A** supports the function of the adrenal glands during chronic stress and protects cells from premature ageing.
   Requirement in stress situations: 5000 IU (approx. 1500 mcg)
   Contained in carrots, tomatoes, apricots, butter, and liver.
   Caution: Pregnant women cannot take vitamin A supplements.

★ B-complex vitamins support the function of the nervous system, have a calming effect, and are important for the processing of proteins and carbohydrates.

Vitamin B-12 improves brain function and aids concentration.

Requirement in stress situations: 100 mcg

Contained in eggs, cheese, and beef.

Vitamin B-6 strengthens the immune system.

Requirement in stress situations: 10 mg

Contained in potatoes, fish, spinach, and chicken.

Vitamin B-2 (riboflavin) protects the organism from stress damage.

Requirement in stress situations: 5 mg

Contained in milk, liver, eggs, fish, and cheese.

★ **Vitamin C** reduces the risk of stress, protects you from infection, and improves your mood.

Requirement in stress situations: 500 mg

Contained in citrus fruits, strawberries, kiwi fruit, bell peppers, blackcurrants, and Brussels sprouts.

★ **Vitamin E** protects blood vessels from the effects of stress, prevents arteriosclerosis, and protects cells from premature ageing.

Requirement in stress situations: 400 IU (approx. 268 mcg)

Contained in vegetable oils, nuts, and wholegrain products.

★ The mineral **magnesium** protects the heart muscle from effects of stress, is calming and relaxing, improves sleep, and prevents muscle cramps.

Requirement in stress situations: 500 mg

Contained in wholegrain products, wheat germ, almonds, nuts, apples, and dark vegetables.

★ The trace element **zinc** strengthens the immune system, which is often affected by stress.

Requirement in stress situations: 15 mg

Contained in fish, mussels, and wheat germ.

You'll find further recommendations for supplementing nutrients in Appendix 3: Our vitamin recommendations for special situations.

Using relaxation breaks to conserve energy

Unfortunately, most of us lack the time to learn important relaxation techniques and then to follow them regularly. But, as a Persian saying goes, 'a moment of peace in your soul is better than anything else you may try to attain.' Often, short moments of relaxation are enough to recharge your energy, so we've put together a few little 'islands of calm' that are relatively easy to work into your daily routine. None of the relaxation methods presented here requires more than five minutes.

If you have more time, we recommend our expanded relaxation programme, described in Appendix 4: Our relaxation programme for those who want to take more time for themselves.

Pets can lower your stress level

The calm observation of fish in an aquarium, says a study performed at the University of Pennsylvania, lowers blood pressure and drives away worries and fears. The slow movement puts the observer in a near-hypnotic state, which has a positive effect on stress levels. Not only do pets relieve the stress of loneliness by providing companionship, but walking the dog on a regular basis gets people out in the sunshine and gently exercising their hearts, while stroking or cuddling pets induces relaxation and consequently lowers blood pressure. In fact, studies have shown that people who own pets of any kind usually have significantly lower blood pressure than those without pets.[34]

Relax in one minute

Rest your elbows on the table and put your hands over your eyes. Clear your mind for 60 seconds and try not to think about anything. If it's hard to turn off your thoughts, concentrate on your breathing. This short exercise refreshes facial muscles and enlivens your mind.

Juggle your stress away

If you really want to get rid of stress, you should learn to juggle. Juggling requires you to relax and concentrate at the same time. There's no room for worrying thoughts when you're dealing with the balls, otherwise they'll end up on the floor. American studies have shown that more endorphins are released when juggling, and stress hormones are dissolved. In the United States, juggling has recently been used as an ideal stress-beating strategy in managing seminars. Letting the balls circle for just five minutes is often enough to turn yourself off and fill up on energy.

Breathe calmly

Stress can literally take our breath away. When worries and frustration take the upper hand, your stomach muscles and diaphragm are cramped, your lungs cannot expand optimally, breathing becomes faster and shallower, and your oxygen supply is worse. Often, only the upper parts of the lungs fill with oxygen-rich air, and a large portion of the lungs is unused. In this type of shallow stress breathing, the shoulders are typically lifted, the chest puffed out, and the stomach is sucked in.

A relaxed person, on the other hand, breathes in and out deeply and slowly. 'Take a deep breath' is therefore a well-meant and very helpful piece of advice whenever stress seems about to bowl us over. Breathing is the only unconscious bodily function that we can also control consciously. In order to use our entire lung capacity, we must breathe with the bottom part of our lungs as well as the upper. This works only when we breathe from the stomach.

In order to practise the right breathing technique, put your hands on your waist, pointing your fingertips towards your navel. Now breathe in so you can feel your stomach moving in and out with your fingers. Avoid lifting your shoulders. Push your stomach out consciously and breathe rhythmically in and out. Deep breathing causes the body to release the calming 'happy hormone' endorphin. Just five or six conscious breaths are often enough to create distance from your stress. The relaxing stomach movement also massages your solar plexus. This web of nerves is found in the upper stomach area and activates the calming parasympathetic nervous system. This dissolves nervous tension and gets rid of uneasiness.

Discover the 'magic touch'

It sounds implausible that you could become noticeably calmer and more balanced in less than a second. But this is the effect of the 'magic touch'. The idea is amazingly simple. Everyone knows about certain pieces of music that call to mind specific pictures and feelings, long thought forgotten, from the subconscious. Memories of a first kiss, a dream holiday, or a great party suddenly return. Smells and gestures can immediately call up positive or negative feelings, too. This phenomenon is known as 'conditioning' in psychology and behavioural science. The best-known example is the dog studied by Russian Ivan Pavlov (1849–1936). In order to condition the animal to a certain stimulus, the scientist rang a bell every time the dog was about to eat. After a short time, the dog began to salivate upon hearing the bell, even when there was nothing to eat. But what does this example have to do with relaxation?

Well, with a little practice, you can use conditioning for quick relaxation. A simple touch is enough to produce peace and well-being. First, think up a 'conditioning touch'. This should be different from your everyday actions. For example, you can rub one earlobe between your fingers or press both thumbs together. For the first step of conditioning, you'll need a little quiet time. Sit down in a comfortable position, breathe regularly, close your eyes, and imagine a situation where you felt very comfortable – a day on holiday, a walk, a childhood experience. Place yourself in that situation. What do you hear? How does the air smell? What are you wearing? As soon as you're completely relaxed and have the scene clearly in your mind, practise your chosen 'magic touch'. Often, one conditioning session is enough to call up this feeling of peace and contentment – through the 'magic touch' – in any situation, be it on the train, at the office, or at home. If necessary, you can repeat this conditioning exercise once more the next day. It's useful to repeat the touch whenever you're very happy and well balanced, in order to strengthen the conditioning. The more often your conditioning touch is associated with pleasant situations, the more intense the relaxing effect will be in an 'emergency'.

Just push the stress away

A couple of practised grips, and you'll be calmness itself even in the most stressful of situations. Acupressure is an excellent way to relax quickly, any time. When applied to certain regions of the body, finger, thumb, and palm pressure have an immediate effect on your circulation and nervous system. An important acupressure point that should be pressed at times of fear or uneasiness is on the lower arm, in line with the middle finger, about two finger widths above your wrist joint, on the underside of your arm. Press this point for several seconds with the thumb of your opposite hand.

Another anti-stress point is on the back of your hand in the triangle of your thumb and index finger. This point is easy to find because it's sensitive to pressure. Massage this point for a few seconds between the thumb and index finger of your other hand until it hurts a little.

Use the power of thought

Close your eyes and imagine a large, fresh, greenish-yellow lemon. You take a knife, cut the fruit open, and bite into it. The sour juice spreads through your mouth. Is your mouth already watering? Then you're one of the people whose body functions can be influenced by the imagination. In more than 90% of Europeans polled, the thought of biting into a lemon activated an increased secretion of saliva.[35] The example shows how easily physical reactions can be provoked by the imagination. Why not use these capabilities to your advantage?

Psychologists have determined that each of us has a subconscious image of him- or herself and lives according to this image.

If you see yourself as a loser, an ignoramus, always in second place, you'll act accordingly and will find that you fail over and over again.

Coach yourself. Several times a day, see yourself in your imagination as a successful winner. Replace negative self-images with positive ones. With the help of the visualisation technique, fears and uncertainties can be removed, and feelings like helplessness improved, as the American Dr Carl Simonton showed many times.[36] Originally, he invented this method to strengthen the immune systems of cancer patients by the power of imagination.

Visualisation exercises can help us influence and strengthen our immune systems. The hormone system, too, can be steered to a certain degree by the 'power of thought'. If you use visualisation exercises regularly, you can reduce tension and influence bodily functions that have been disturbed by stress, such as your heartbeat and breathing.

Lie or sit down comfortably, close your eyes, and breathe in and out, in and out, very calmly. Imagine a billowing cornfield that's moving in rhythm with your breathing. Relax and loosen all your muscles one by one. Begin with your face and go through all the muscle groups down to your feet. When you're completely relaxed, let the problems and situations that are troubling you appear before your inner eye as pictures. Watch as the pictures slowly move away, growing smaller and less important and finally disappearing on the horizon. Imagine yourself as self-confident and successful.

Roll back the tension

There are several reflex points on the foot that can have a relaxing effect, too. With the help of a tennis ball, you can massage them very easily.

Take off your shoes and socks and place a tennis ball under the arch of your foot. Put just enough weight on the ball so that the pressure is still comfortable, and move your foot back and forth. The pressure stimulates nerve endings, which use the reflexes to release tension in many parts of the body.

Summary

★ Stress is the most commonly occurring health-risk factor in our society. Not only does it steal important life energy, but it also promotes various common illnesses (heart attack, cancer).

★ In stressful situations, the adrenal glands release increased amounts of the hormones adrenaline, noradrenaline, and cortisol. These accelerate the metabolism. Heart rate and blood pressure increase, and calorie use increases by 15%. The organism ages faster, and life expectancy is reduced.

★ Patience and 'laziness' are recommended as countermeasures. This type of behaviour can only be realised through a new lifestyle and directed relaxation exercises.

Chapter Five

Sleepyheads get more out of life

Chapter Five

5

'Sleep, all things' rest: Sleep, gentlest of the gods, the spirit's peace, care flies from within, who soothes the body wearied with toil, and readies it for fresh labours'

— Ovid (43 BC–c. AD 18), Roman poet

This chapter covers:
- ★ **why sleep is a fountain of youth**
- ★ **why you shouldn't get up before 7:20 am**
- ★ **how your hormones are influenced by sleep**
- ★ **why lack of sleep makes you old, stupid, ill, and fat**

Late sleepers – cooking over a low flame

To anyone who's ever had a guilty conscience because they slept in until 11:00 am, you can breathe easy. Abundant sleep is not only healthy, but it also protects your valuable life energy, strengthens your immune system, and keeps you young longer. While we're asleep, our bodies switch to low power. The digestive system rests, muscles loosen, body temperature drops, and breathing becomes slower and deeper than during the day when we're awake.

The level of cortisol, a stress hormone, reaches its lowest point at night. While you're sleeping, the brain processes and stores information taken in during the day. The entire organism is able to recuperate. Saving energy, however, is one of the most important reasons to get enough sleep. While you sleep, your metabolism is less active and your calorie use is lower. If you sleep one extra hour a day, you save at least 50 calories. Over ten years, this means that a longer sleeper saves nearly 200,000 calories of life energy.

Hibernation keeps animals refreshed

In animals, the life-lengthening effects of sleep are easy to demonstrate. Animals that spend a large part of the day dozing and sleeping generally have a higher life expectancy. Compare the behaviour of dogs and cats. House cats often lie in wait for hours at a time and spend most of the rest of the day sleeping. Slumbering peacefully, they can live for up to 20 years and sometimes more.

Dogs, on the other hand, are much more active, particularly wild dogs. They live in a pack, establish hierarchies, and chase after their prey. As a result, dogs rarely live to be more than 15 years old.

This effect is even clearer in mammals that hibernate, nearly halting their energy use for months at a time. They live significantly longer than animals that are active year-round. While mice, which do not hibernate, live to be only three or four years old, bats of approximately the same size and weight can live up to 30 years. The reason for these differing life expectancies is the hibernation regularly taken by bats.

Similar observations can be made of other animals that hibernate.

Lack of sleep makes you old, stupid, ill, and fat

The average length of sleep for people in the developed world has reduced from 9 hours, in 1910, to 7.5. In all likelihood, we will sleep even less in the years to come. A well-regarded study by Eve van Cauter's research team at the University of Chicago shows how a chronic lack of sleep can be harmful for humans. This 1999 study, published in the renowned medical journal *The Lancet*, observed a group of healthy young men in a sleep laboratory. They were allowed only four hours of sleep a night. After just a week, sleep deprivation had thrown their hormone regulation and metabolism into confusion. In particular, the hormone insulin, which is normally released by the pancreas and protects us from diabetes, could no longer regulate their blood sugar levels. Within a week, sleep deprivation had put the men into a state usually found only in older people or people in the early stages of diabetes. On the basis of the study's data, van Cauter speculates that chronic lack of sleep can cause or worsen age-related diseases like diabetes, obesity, high blood pressure, and memory loss. Additionally, bad moods, problems with concentration, and even depression can result from sleep deprivation.[37]

Relaxed after 7:20 am

A recent discovery by British researchers provides music to the ears of late sleepers: if you get up later, you'll be more relaxed and patient throughout the rest of the day. As reported in a 1999 issue of the magazine *New Scientist*, early risers are significantly more stressed than late sleepers. Researchers at London's Westminster University measured much higher levels of the stress hormone cortisol in the saliva of people who got up before 7:20 am than in those who didn't get out of bed until later. Going to bed earlier doesn't seem to help. The total amount of sleep, according to the British scientists, didn't have any influence on the stress hormone's release.[38] Whether subjects were stressed or relaxed depended solely on the time they got up.

The stress of early rising does not just affect the rest of the day, but can even have serious consequences for overall health, says the report. Long periods of chronic stress can lead to depression; the immune system is weakened; and in addition, early risers are much more likely to suffer from infections, muscle pains, and bad moods.

What is true for adults is even more the case for children and adolescents. A research team led by Epstein, a sleep researcher from Israel, studied more than 800 Israeli schoolchildren between the ages of 10 and 11. While some had to get up at 7:15 am, the others were able to sleep until 8:00 am. Even though their alarm clocks were set only 45 minutes apart, the early risers were much more likely to suffer from daytime fatigue and had problems concentrating.[39] As a result, more and more sleep researchers are lobbying for a later-starting school day.

How the body reacts to sleep and relaxation

★ Blood pressure sinks to its normal level, which should be under 140/90 mmHg.

★ After a half-hour break, the heart reaches its resting pulse.

★ After about ten minutes of relaxation, oxygen use decreases and breathing slows. Breathing decreases from 40 breaths when stressed to 12 while sleeping.

★ Fewer stress hormones are produced in your sleep, and the rejuvenating hormone melatonin is released.

Become younger in your sleep

Here is another argument for being a 'sleepyhead': you become younger while sleeping. This effect is caused by the sleep hormone melatonin. It prepares the body for the night's sleep: blood pressure drops, your heart beats more slowly, your eyes grow heavy. But this hormone can do more than make you sleepy. It has been proven in various studies that melatonin has a rejuvenating effect and can lengthen life. When this hormone was added to mice's food or drinking water, they lived 20 to 30% longer than the mice in the control group that did not receive the hormone. When older mice received transplants of the pineal gland – that is, the gland that produces melatonin – of younger mice, the elderly rodents outlived their contemporaries by up to 50%. The exact mechanism of this sleep hormone has not yet been explained. Possibly, melatonin saves energy by promoting longer and more restorative sleep.

Sleep affects body temperature and metabolism

Another rejuvenating effect of sleep is the slowing of the metabolic processes caused by sinking body temperature. The sleep hormone melatonin, which puts you into a deep, refreshing sleep at night, also lowers body temperature during the night.

This in turn results in reduced metabolic activity and decreased energy use. The difference in daytime and nighttime body temperature is particularly great in young people, who sleep more deeply. In older people, who generally sleep worse and for shorter amounts of time, and who often produce only small amounts of the sleep hormone, body temperature drops much less. The body temperature of good sleepers reaches its lowest point about 4–5 hours after they fall asleep.

Produce your own anti-ageing hormones

We take in the amino acid tryptophan with our food. During the day, our bodies use this to create the messenger serotonin. As soon as it gets dark – the pineal gland is connected to the outside world through the optic nerve – serotonin is converted into the sleep hormone melatonin. The hormone melatonin is produced in the pineal gland, a tiny gland in the centre of the brain.

Research is still being carried out, but the sleep hormone melatonin has been shown to serve the following purposes:

★ It's an effective antioxidant; that is, it protects cells from damage and ageing processes.
★ It increases our immune system's capabilities.
★ It lowers body temperature at night and leads to a lower level of energy use.
★ It postpones the ageing process.

How to stimulate the production of melatonin

1 Eat food in the afternoon and evening that contains large amounts of tryptophan, which provides the fuel for melatonin production:

★ soya beans   ★ poultry (especially turkey)

★ bananas   ★ lamb

★ peas   ★ pasta

★ pineapple   ★ eggs

★ beans   ★ nuts

2 Relax! After just 30 minutes of sleep and relaxation, more melatonin is released.

Guidelines for a revitalising sleep

At least one in ten people suffers from sleep disturbances; some estimates even say that one in three people has an occasional restless night. Often, sleep training and appropriate sleep hygiene can solve the problem – because you can learn and practise how to sleep right.

Sleep seldom does what you want it to

The famous Viennese psychiatrist Viktor Frankl (1905–1997) had an unusual way of treating patients who couldn't sleep. Patients who wanted Frankl to treat them had to make an appointment with him by phone. In cases of sleep disturbance, Frankl regularly did the following: he told the patient on the other end of the line that he wouldn't have an appointment free for another week. In the meantime, however, the patient could do something that would go a long way toward correcting the problem, and which would help the therapy work faster. On the phone, Frankl gave the patients the assignment of keeping a record of their sleep habits until the time of their appointment. Each hour during the night, they were to make a note of whether they had slept or not. The patients were excited about this suggestion and began taking notes the very next night. To their surprise, they determined that whenever they weren't supposed to go to sleep (in order to fill out the protocol as required), they couldn't stay awake and slept the whole night through. At the appointment time, they often appeared quite upset, and told the psychiatrist that, bizarre as it sounds, after several years of insomnia they had suddenly been able to sleep well during the test week.[40]

You, too, can trick your subconscious: try to stay awake for an especially long time tonight and try not to go to sleep no matter what. In most cases it won't work, and you'll fall asleep surprisingly early.

Make sure you have the right environment

The bedroom should be the quietest room in the house and should, therefore, be located as far away from the street as possible. It should also be well ventilated, but not too cold. Especially in the wintertime – contrary to popular belief – it's not ideal to sleep with the window open. When the room temperature sinks too low, your body needs a lot of energy to maintain body temperature – which disturbs your refreshing sleep. The ideal sleeping temperature is approximately 18°C (64°F).

Don't skimp on your bed. Good, high-quality mattresses are a must for a relaxing sleep and are a basic requirement for saving energy. A too-small bed and a shared mattress, on the other hand, prevent long deep-sleep phases; every sleeper moves more than thirty times a night and can disturb his or her partner's restful sleep.

The one-minute nap
The body recovers while you sleep and gains new strength. While it regenerates, your mind can rest. In the long term, most people are productive only when they sleep an average of eight hours or more a night; you should allow your body this time on a regular basis.

However, a one-minute nap can give you a quick refill of energy. Though it may sound unbelievable at first, this short creative break is more useful than a half-hour afternoon nap. Although most people who have mastered the art of the afternoon nap wake up feeling refreshed, many people actually feel more tired after a longer nap.

Here's how to do it:

Sit in a chair with your feet firmly on the floor and rest your elbows/lower arms on your knees while holding on to your key ring. Let your head hang down. Try to shut yourself off. With a little practice, if you're fairly tired you'll instantly fall into a brief sleep. The key ring is your alarm clock; as soon as you fall asleep, your muscles will relax, and the keys will fall to the floor, ensuring that you don't really fall asleep – because while this brief sleep provides a burst of energy, a short nap will only make you feel more tired.

As you eat, so shall you sleep

If your stomach spends the night fighting with your evening pork chop, large pizza, or three-course meal, you won't be able to sleep well.

A light dinner, conversely, can actually promote falling asleep. Carbohydrates are calming and balancing, and promote sleep. The group of carbohydrates includes pasta, bread, rice, potatoes, and fruit. Fatty foods like fried things and large portions of meat are hard to digest and keep the digestive system busy for several hours.

Protein-rich foods in particular, including meat, cheese, and dairy products, generally counteract tiredness.

It depends, however, on the protein composition of the foods. Foods that contain the protein building block tyrosine are sleep-stealers, because the protein material is turned into activating, stimulating hormones (dopamine, norepinephrine). You should therefore only eat these foods during the daytime.

Eat the following tyrosine-rich foods in the morning and during the day to help yourself stay awake:

★ wholegrain bread and cereals
★ low fat milk
★ cheese
★ tofu
★ yogurt
★ lean meat
★ fish
★ eggs
★ legumes

In the evening, you need tryptophan-rich foods. The protein building block tryptophan is converted into the sleep hormone melatonin, which gives us good, refreshing sleep.

Eat the following tryptophan-rich foods in the evening to help you sleep:

★ poultry (especially turkey)
★ carbohydrate-rich fruit and dried fruits (bananas, pineapple, dates, figs)
★ nuts
★ all kinds of pasta
★ seafood
★ soya products

Alcohol – a sleeping potion?

You may like to drink a glass of beer or wine in the evening to put you to sleep. It's true that alcohol makes you tired and helps you go to sleep. However, highly alcoholic drinks affect your sleep later. Deep-sleep phases in particular are disturbed by alcohol with the result being that despite getting enough sleep, you don't feel refreshed and renewed when you wake up.

Attention: 'waking potions'

If you have trouble sleeping, you should avoid coffee, cola, and black tea, starting in the afternoon. Caffeine, even that found in green tea, is a stimulant that can influence people's sleep hours later. It has an activating effect and isn't helpful in putting you to sleep. Be careful with chocolate too. It contains caffeine-like substances that have a stimulant effect and make you more awake. Chilli peppers and other spicy foods should also be avoided at bedtime by those who have sleep problems. The hormone capsaicin, which makes peppers spicy, makes us awake and active because it jumpstarts the metabolism and raises blood pressure.

Caution: television!

Suspense films and exciting football games can lead to physical stress reactions. Films can be just as exciting as real life (and often more so). The borders between reality and fiction are temporarily erased, and the film you expected to be relaxing causes physical stress with all its symptoms: higher blood pressure, increased heartbeat and breathing rate, and perspiration. Stress hormones are even released, preparing us for a battle with the fictitious enemy – but we stay rooted in our easy chairs. Still, suspense films aren't all bad. They can hold our attention so well that we forget about everyday stresses. Our thoughts are distracted, and everyday problems suddenly seem small.

Whether we wake up refreshed or exhausted the morning after a TV marathon depends on how we process what we've seen and whether the suspense created by the film can be dispelled once it's over. An evening stroll is ideal for getting rid of stress after watching the show.

Stroll into sleep

On the way to work, we're usually sitting in the car or on the train, and during the workday most of us are more or less chained to our desks for eight hours or so. At home, we sit down to a nice dinner and then lie on the sofa and watch TV – no wonder many people can't get to sleep at night.

Since we hardly move all day, we don't have any opportunity to dissolve stress hormones and set our bodies right. An evening stroll is ideal for shaking off the day's tension before bedtime.

Moderate doses of exercise decrease stress-hormone levels and cause increased numbers of 'happy hormones,' endorphins, to be released. This calms the nerves and improves your sleep.

If you follow a regular relaxing exercise programme like peripatetic meditation (see pages 37–38), you'll reduce your stress level, and in the future it will be easier to remain calm in difficult situations. Vigorous athletic exercise, on the other hand, is no good in the evening. The effort activates your circulatory system, and your tiredness is driven away.

Harder physical exertion should therefore be done at least four hours before bedtime.

Find peace with the right music

Lullabies exist in almost every culture. Primitive people put themselves in a trancelike state with monotonous rhythms; children are still sung to sleep, and in some supermarkets music creates a relaxed shopping atmosphere. We've known for a long time that music is a fantastic way to relax and help us go to sleep. The Russian ambassador to Germany, Count Hermann Carl von Keyserling (1696–1764) had several pieces composed for him by Johann Sebastian Bach as therapy for his troubling sleep disturbances, and a musician was always on hand to play the compositions.

The effect of music on the psyche and the body has been researched thoroughly. Regular body rhythms like breathing, heartbeat, and brain waves tend to adapt themselves to music tempo.

However, the hormone system, blood pressure, and the immune system can also be positively influenced by the right music. Research has shown that, in particular, music whose tempo is slower than your heartbeat can have a calming and soporific effect. Music pieces in 'largo', especially, can affect measurable levels of relaxation.

We have found that the following pieces of Western classical music are particularly well suited for relaxation and for promoting sleep (people with different musical tastes and cultural backgrounds should substitute their own choices):

Johann Sebastian Bach
★ Largo from Piano Concerto No. 5 in F Minor, BWV 1056
★ Largo from Flute Concerto in G Minor, BWV 1056
★ Aria from the *Goldberg Variations*, BWV 988

Georg Frederick Handel
★ All the slow passages from Concerti Grossi Op. 6, Nos. 1 to 12
★ Largo from Concerto No. 3 in D Major *(Music for the Royal Fireworks)*

Antonio Vivaldi
★ Largo from 'Winter' – *The Four Seasons*
★ Largo from Concerto in D Major for guitar, strings, and figured bass

Frédéric Chopin
★ Any of the *Nocturnes*

Franz Schubert
★ Symphony No. 8 in B minor ('Unfinished')

Wolfgang Amadeus Mozart
★ Andante from *Eine Kleine Nachtmusik*

If you don't have a classical music library, it's a good idea to search the Internet or look in record shops for CDs of pre-selected collections of music, both classical and non-classical, designed for relaxation, healing, or meditation.

Summary

★ Deeper and longer sleep is an important prerequisite for physical and mental fitness. Sleep helps you recuperate. The body saves life energy. Animals that sleep a lot or hibernate live longer than those that sleep only a little.

★ Many people sleep less than seven hours a night during the working week.[41] This is far too little. Even a division of the day into eight hours of work, eight hours of free time, and eight hours of sleep is not enough for most people to jump out of bed in a good mood. It should be eight hours *at the very least.*

★ It's important how long you sleep, as well as what time you get up. If you regularly get up before 7:20 am, you'll have more stress hormones in your body all day than a late riser will. Stress hormones disturb productivity and thinking capability.

★ You can learn how to sleep right. A healthy sleep requires certain parameters. These include: successful stress management; the right environment (room, temperature, bed); and sleep-encouraging eating behaviour (no stimulating foods or drinks, and no hard-to-digest foods at dinner).

Chapter Six

Sun and heat – the fountains of youth

6

'Whoever wishes to investigate medicine properly, should proceed thus: in the first place to consider the seasons of the year, and what effects each of them produces.'

— Hippocrates (460–377 BC), Greek physician

This chapter covers:
- ★ **why southern Europeans live longer than northern Europeans**
- ★ **why cold showers waste your life energy**
- ★ **how you can save energy with warmth**
- ★ **why you should spend winters in warm climates**

Why heat helps you conserve energy

Did you know that, on average, Italians and Greeks live longer than northern Europeans? Until now this has been put down to the Mediterranean diet, with its large quantities of fruit and vegetables, lots of olive oil, and plenty of red wine. Certainly diet plays an important role, but there's probably another, less noticed advantage that southern Europeans have over their northern neighbours: warmth and sunlight. Regardless of the outside temperature, our bodies maintain a temperature of about 37°C (98.6°F). When outside temperatures drop, the body must heat up more in order to keep its temperature constant. The metabolism works overtime, which naturally costs us more energy. The increase in heat production uses up an extra-large serving of calories. We unconsciously adjust our eating habits to our seasonal needs and take in more calories in the winter than in the warmer summer months. In the winter, we instinctively eat fattier and more carbohydrate-filled foods. But it's not just warmth that plays an important role in this. Sunlight, too, has a positive influence on our bodies. It affects our hormone system, has a positive effect on the metabolism and the immune system, reduces appetite, and can lower blood pressure.

Careful, human beings aren't cold-blooded animals

Maybe you're surprised that we're recommending warmth for saving energy. You may already have heard the theory that cold temperatures preserve the body. You probably still remember learning in chemistry class that many biological processes run faster with more heat, thereby increasing energy use. It follows that cold should slow these processes down and save metabolic energy. Fish, for example, live longer in cool water. Fruit flies live longer in rooms with lower temperatures than in their normal environment.

But these results aren't as easily transferred to humans as is commonly assumed. What is being overlooked is that fish are cold-blooded. They have no trouble adapting their body temperature to their surroundings. If the surrounding temperature drops, the fish's temperature drops; metabolic processes happen more slowly, and energy is saved. It's very different in human beings. The warm-blooded human being depends on the fact that his or her inner temperature remains at a fairly constant 37°C (98.6°F). In contrast to the fish, the human body uses up all its energy reserves to keep body temperature constant – which naturally costs us a lot of calories.

In the winter, our hormone system suffers from stress

Our hormone system works differently in the winter than in the summer. Maintaining body temperature in cold weather is a priority for the body. The sympathetic (or impulse-causing) nervous system, which also turns on in times of stress, is very active in the winter. In order to stimulate metabolism, thereby producing more warmth, the adrenal glands release more fight-or-flight stress hormones (cortisol, adrenaline, and norepinephrine) in the winter – as well as in a cold shower. These hormones provide the body with extra energy reserves. The thyroid gland, too, produces more thyroid hormones in cold weather in order to heat up the body's furnace and maintain body temperature. The stress and thyroid hormones cause our basic fuel needs to rise, burning more calories. A walk in cold weather uses up about 50 more calories per hour than it does in the summer. This 'heating up' costs our organism extra life energy.

Lowering your blood pressure with heat

Studies have shown the positive effects of nudism, and particularly nude sunbathing, on blood pressure.[42] Further studies showed that even sunbathing can slightly lower your blood pressure.[43] This effect is much more noticeable in people with high blood pressure. In an experiment, sunbathing lowered their blood pressure by more than twice as much as it did in people with normal blood pressure.[44] The effect lasted for almost a week. The blood-pressure-lowering effect is probably due to the mild warmth of the sun; blood vessels expand and pressure drops.

The influence of the sun may also be a factor in the production of as-yet undetected blood-pressure-lowering agents. But be careful: people with extremely high blood pressure should enjoy the effects of milder temperatures only. On very hot days, sunbathing and high temperatures present a great strain on these people's circulatory systems.

Sunlight creates a feeling of well-being
Many people have an ambivalent relationship to the sun. On the one hand we love being outside in the summer, enjoying the warmth, lazing around in deck chairs, and enjoying the good mood that

comes with a sunny day. On the other hand, our fear of the sun's harmful effects is growing more and more. But the same is true for sunbathing as for most things in life: whether something is helpful or harmful often depends on the dosage. Enjoyed in moderation, the positive health benefits of sunlight outweigh the negative. In sunlight, our serotonin levels rise. This transmitter causes even-temperedness and good moods. Symptoms of stress disappear. Additionally, under the influence of serotonin the desire for sweets decreases – therefore, it's easier to reduce your calorie intake in the summer.

How to save life energy with heat

From the perspective of Metabolic Theory, it makes sense to spend winters in warm climates. The warm temperature prevents our organism from having to go into winter's high gear. In addition, it's easier for us to stick to our reduced-calorie, high-in-fruit-and-vegetables diet in nice warm weather. The third reason why a winter trip – or, even better, a 'migration' – to a warm climate can lengthen your life and improve your health and productivity is that you'll be in a better mood. In a dark northern winter, the number of people who suffer from depression increases dramatically. When your mood is dark, your body releases more of the harmful stress hormone cortisol, which, as we've already mentioned, makes us age faster, harms the brain, and weakens the immune system.

If you can't plan a change of scenery in the winter months, make sure you heat your office and home well in order to lower your body's energy use. Turn the heater up to 22°C (72°F) or wear warm clothes to conserve life energy.

In freezing temperatures, you shouldn't sleep with the windows open. When the room is too cold, your metabolism shifts into high gear in order to avoid heat loss. If the temperature in your bedroom drops below 15°C (59°F), your sleep will grow increasingly less restful and less refreshing, since your body is constantly trying to heat itself up as protection from the cold. During a cold night, metabolic rates can be so high that we start to sweat under the covers despite the cold – an indication of the amounts of energy that this supposedly healthy sleep in the cold is costing us. Aside from increased calorie use because of the cold, we're also missing out on the energy we would normally conserve by sleeping restfully.

Even the much-lauded cold shower in the morning isn't necessarily good for our health. The cold water is like a shock to the body. Numerous studies have shown that our bodies react to this as they do to other stresses: the cold shower leads to a massive release of the stress hormone cortisol and stimulates energy use. If you want to save energy while showering, you should choose a warmer temperature.

Tips on how to stay warm and save energy
★ Travel to warm climates in the winter.
★ If you stay in a cold climate during the winter, you should heat rooms to about 22°C (72°F).
★ The temperature in your bedroom shouldn't fall below 15°C (59°F).
★ Don't sleep with the windows open in the winter.
★ Take only warm showers.
★ Reduce your exposure to cold everywhere else as well.

Summary

★ In cold temperatures, the body releases more stress hormones, which accelerate the metabolism. At the same time, you require more energy to maintain a constant body temperature.
★ In warm temperatures, energy use decreases and the production of stress hormones sinks. The body switches over to energy-saving mode.
★ In mild temperatures, high blood pressure drops and the strain is taken off your circulatory system.

Appendices

Appendix 1

Our recommendations for peripatetic meditation and the brisk walk

Exercise . . .

★ **. . . regularly**. Four 30-minute sessions a week are ideal. In this way the training can take effect on both body and psyche. After only four weeks of this moderate training, you'll notice that you are calmer in your everyday life and better able to deal with stress.

★ **. . . moderately**. Performance-oriented, ambitious training and relaxation are mutually exclusive. Don't push yourself so hard that your pulse exceeds 120 bpm. Your tempo should be slow enough that you have sufficient breath to carry on a conversation. Choose a flat area to start with so that your meditation isn't distracted by changing intensity of the exercise.

★ **. . . without tension**. Getting in a lap before work or dashing to the gym on your lunch break may be impressive, but it has nothing to do with relaxation. When you're under time pressure, physical exercise can quickly become yet another stress factor. Plan regular, fixed times and give yourself long enough for a little exercise. If, every so often, you don't have time to exercise, skip your session rather than rushing through it. This should not, of course, become a habit. If you have to skip more than two exercise sessions a month, you should revise your schedule.

★ **. . . enjoyably**. Exercise should be fun for you; this increases its positive effects. With peripatetic meditation, the meditative effect is an aspect of this.

★ **. . . with the proper equipment**. Beginner athletes don't need any expensive equipment at first. For peripatetic meditation, you should make sure you have good shoes. For outdoor training, it's important to have breathable clothing that draws away sweat and prevents overheating.

★ **. . . while well nourished**. Physical activity increases your vitamin, mineral, and trace element requirements. Pay special attention to having a balanced diet. Our recommendations for nutrient supplements can be found in Appendix 3.

Appendix 2

The proper weight for adults

The weights listed below are average weights for people over 25 years old, without clothing. Please note that average weights vary based on a person's body type and age.[45]

WOMEN		MEN	
HEIGHT (IN)	WEIGHT (LBS)	HEIGHT (IN)	WEIGHT (LBS)
59	93.5–113.5	63	119.0–139.0
59.5	96.0–115.5	63.5	121.5–141.0
60	98.0–118.0	64	124.5–144.5
60.5	100.0–121.0	64.5	126.5–148.0
61	103.0–124.0	65	129.0–150.0
61.5	105.0–127.0	65.5	131.0–153.0
62	107.0–129.0	66	134.0–158.0
62.5	109.0–132.0	66.5	136.5–160.0
63	112.0–135.5	67	139.0–162.0
63.5	114.5–139.0	67.5	141.0–164.5
64	117.0–142.0	68	144.5–168.5
64.5	119.0–145.5	68.5	146.5–171.0
65	121.5–148.0	69	149.0–173.5
65.5	123.5–150.0	69.5	151.0–177.0
66	127.0–153.0	70	154.0–180.0
66.5	129.0–154.5	70.5	156.5–183.0
67	131.0–159.0	71	159.0–185.0
67.5	133.5–161.0	71.5	161.0–187.5
68	136.5–165.0	72	164.0–191.5
68.5	139.0–167.5	72.5	166.5–194.0
69	140.5–170.0	73	169.5–197.5
69.5	142.5–173.0	73.5	171.0–200.5
70	146.5–177.5	74	174.0–203.5
70.5	148.0–180.0	74.5	176.5–206.5
71	150.0–182.0	75	179.0–209.5

71.5	152.0–184.0	75.5	181.0–210.5
72	155.0–188.0	76	184.0–215.0
72.5	157.5–190.5	76.5	186.5–217.0
73	159.0–193.0	77	188.5–220.0

Your Body Mass Index (BMI)

The table above differs somewhat from the standard BMI chart that is considered to be the 'measurement of choice' by many researchers who study obesity, so we have included this as well.

Calculating BMI

★ Determine your height in inches (e.g., 5 feet 5 inches = 65 inches)
★ Square that number (65 x 65 = 4225)
★ Divide your weight in pounds by the result (e.g., 140 ÷ 4225 = 0.0331)
★ Multiply that number by 703 (0.0331 x 703 = 23.27)

For middle-aged adults, a BMI between 20 and 27 falls within the desirable range; a BMI over 27 indicates overweight; and a BMI above 29 indicates obesity. Children and pregnant women have different BMI guidelines. (The World Health Organization's classification of what represents normal, overweight, and obese for the overall adult population is marginally different: a normal BMI is between 18.5 and 24.9; overweight is between 25 and 29.9; and obese is over 30.)

The BMI is an improvement over other weight/height tables because it's based on an individual's body mass rather than on a sample of people, but it still doesn't provide a measure of the fatness or leanness of the body. To do that, one's body-fat content must be assessed.

Table of Body Mass Indexes[46]

BMI (KG/M²)	19	20	21	22	23	24	25	26	27	28	29	30	35	40
HEIGHT (IN)	BODY WEIGHT (LBS)													
58	91	96	100	105	110	115	119	124	129	134	138	143	167	191
59	94	99	104	109	114	119	124	128	133	138	143	148	173	198
60	97	102	107	112	118	123	128	133	138	143	148	153	179	204
61	100	106	111	116	122	127	132	137	143	148	153	158	185	211

62	104	109	115	120	126	131	136	142	147	153	158	164	191	218
63	107	113	118	124	130	135	141	146	152	158	163	169	197	225
64	110	116	122	128	134	140	145	151	157	163	169	174	204	232
65	114	120	126	132	138	144	150	156	162	168	174	180	210	240
66	118	124	130	136	142	148	155	161	167	173	179	186	216	247
67	121	127	134	140	146	153	159	166	172	178	185	191	223	255
68	125	131	138	144	151	158	164	171	177	184	190	197	230	262
69	128	135	142	149	155	162	169	176	182	189	196	203	236	270
70	132	139	146	153	160	167	174	181	188	195	202	207	243	278
71	136	143	150	157	165	172	179	186	193	200	208	215	250	286
72	140	147	154	162	169	177	184	191	199	206	213	221	258	294
73	144	151	159	166	174	182	189	197	204	212	219	227	265	302
74	148	155	163	171	179	186	194	202	210	218	225	233	272	311
75	152	160	168	176	184	192	200	208	216	224	232	240	279	319
76	156	164	172	180	189	197	205	213	221	230	238	246	287	328

Appendix 3

Our vitamin recommendations for special situations

ATTENTION:

If you decide to use more than one of the vitamin combinations described below, please do NOT add the amounts of individual vitamins, minerals, and trace elements, but instead choose the highest recommended dose for each one.

PROTECTION OF CELLS	
vitamin C	500 mg
vitamin E	400 IU
vitamin A	5000 IU
selenium	50 mcg
zinc	12 mg

PROTECTION FROM BONE DECAY (OSTEOPOROSIS)	
calcium	1000 mg
vitamin D	300 IU

PROTECTION FROM ARTERIOSCLEROSIS (IMPORTANT FOR THOSE WITH HIGH CHOLESTEROL, DIABETES, OR STRESS)	
vitamin C	500 mg
beta-carotene	20,000 IU
vitamin E	300 IU
selenium	50 mcg
vitamin B-3 (Niacin)	60 mg

vitamin B-6	10 mg
vitamin B-12	10 mcg
folic acid	600 mcg
chromium	200 mcg

DIABETES MELLITUS (HIGH BLOOD SUGAR LEVEL)

chromium	200 mcg
magnesium	400 mg
zincorotate	12 mg

STRENGTHENING THE IMMUNE SYSTEM

vitamin C	500 mg
vitamin E	600 IU
vitamin A	5000 IU
beta-carotene	20,000 IU
selenium	100 mcg
zincorotate	15 mg
chromium	200 mcg

Appendix 4

Our relaxation programme for those who want to take more time for themselves

Lie down in a comfortable position on your back, on the sofa, in bed, or on the floor. Let your arms rest next to your body and try to relax all of your muscles. Close your eyes.

★ First concentrate on the muscles in your lower arms, paying attention to the tension there. Now imagine that these muscles are gradually relaxing and getting looser and looser. As soon as these muscles are completely relaxed, which can take up to a minute at first, move on to the next muscle group.

★ Now concentrate on the muscles in your upper arms. Pay attention to the tension in these muscles, too. Again, imagine that these muscles are gradually relaxing and getting looser and looser. As soon as the tension in these muscles has gone away, compare your relaxed upper-arm muscles with the lower arm muscles you relaxed earlier. As soon as the relaxation level in both muscle groups is equal, and you have the feeling that all your arm muscles are well relaxed, move on to the next muscle group.

★ Now concentrate on your facial muscles. Here, too, you'll be able to feel a certain tension. Imagine that the tension is flowing out of your muscles, and your facial muscles become soft and pliable. The muscles in your forehead, eyes, and mouth will be very loose and relaxed. As soon as your facial muscles are well relaxed, compare the relaxation in your face with the state of your previously relaxed muscles. If you still feel a little tension in your face, release it by imagining the tension draining away from the muscles. Make sure that the rest of your already relaxed muscles stay relaxed during this exercise. Change to the next muscle group as soon as your facial muscles are well relaxed.

★ Now concentrate on your neck muscles. Relax this muscle group as you did the others. Pay attention to lingering tensions here, too, and compare the neck's state of relaxation to that of the other muscle groups. Do not move on to the next muscle group until you're sure that all the previously relaxed muscles are still relaxed.

★ Now concentrate on your chest and lateral back muscles. These are very broad muscles, so you should first locate the tensions in them and then loosen the individual muscles bit by bit by imagining each one and picturing each muscle relax as the tension fades away. The fastest way to reach a deep state of relaxation is to concentrate first on the left side of your chest, then the right, and then the left and right sides of your back. Give yourself plenty of time to relax this muscle group and don't move on to the next muscle group until you're sure all the muscles in your chest and back are completely relaxed and loosened. During this phase, don't forget to check the state of all your previously relaxed muscles, possibly working out any remaining tensions.

★ The next muscle group you will concentrate on is the stomach muscles. Here, too, you will find only slight tensions at first. Imagine that you are gradually loosening these knots, and that your stomach muscles are becoming soft and pliable. Concentrate on any remaining tension and don't move on to the next muscle group until you're sure that all tension has disappeared from the stomach muscles. Make sure that all of the previously relaxed muscles continue to be relaxed.

★ Now turn your attention to your leg muscles. These are the last muscles you need to relax. Since these muscles have varying functions, you should try to differentiate between them, at least while you're learning, and not try to relax all of the muscles at once. First turn to the muscles on the front side of your thighs; once these are relaxed, concentrate on the backs of your thighs. Treat them the same way as you did the other muscles. Now move on to the muscles in your lower legs. Concentrate first on your calves, then on your shin muscles. Let all the tension flow out of your legs, and when you've finished, check the state of all your other muscles again. If you detect any residual traces of tension in a muscle or muscle group, try to eliminate it as you did the others.

★ Now you are well relaxed. Deepen this state of relaxation by breathing in and out regularly, imagining with every breath that you're becoming more and more relaxed. Remain lying down for a few minutes, then return to the world. Stretch out your arms and legs. Breathe deeply in and out. Open your eyes.

Endnotes

1 *Welt am Sonntag,* March 1990.

2 R. Walford, *Maximum Life Span* (New York: W.W. Norton & Co., 1985).

3 Wilhelm Busch (1832–1908), the great German author and artist, is also considered one of the founders of the comic strip.

4 The Gallup Organization website, www.gallup.com/subscription/ ?m=f&c_id=12945: 'Americans rate family and health as the two most important aspects of their lives, among nine included in a recent Gallup Poll' (January 2003).

5 H. Franke, *Auf den Spuren der Langlebigkeit* (Stuttgart, Germany: F.K. Schattauer Verlag, 1985). [Franke, a medical doctor who worked at the University of Würzburg, Germany, studied elderly people and analysed their lifestyles.]

6 R.S. Paffenbarger, et al., 'Physical activity, all-cause mortality and longevity of college alumni', *New England Journal of Medicine* 314 (1986): 605; B.A. Stamford and P. Shimer, *Fitness Without Exercise* (New York: Warner Books, 1990), 10–11.

7 D.B. Jacoby, 'Physical activity and longevity of college alumni', *New England Journal of Medicine* 315 (1986): 399; see also *Fitness Without Exercise* for more information.

8 H. Meerman, 'Gedächtnisstörungen bei älteren Marathonläufern', *Max Planck Gesellschaft zur Förderung der Wissenschaften-Spiegel* (April 1995), 13–14; H. Meerman 'Ältere Marathonläufer leben unter Stress; *Max Planck Gesellschaft zur Förderung der Wissenschaften-Spiegel* (January 1992), 3–4.

9 K.H. Cooper, *Dr Kenneth H. Cooper's Antioxidant Revolution* (Nashville, TN: Thomas Nelson, 1994).

10 'Olympia-Übersicht: Feten, Tränen und Romanzen', *Fuldaer Zeitung,* 1 September 2000.

11 U. Müller, 'Der plötzliche Tod beim Marathonlauf', *Die Welt,* 12 September 2000.

12 A.P. Polednak, 'College athletics, body size and cancer mortality', *Cancer* 38 (1976): 382–387.

13 R.S. Paffenbarger, et al., 'Physical activity, all-cause mortality, and longevity of college alumni', *New England Journal of Medicine* 314 (1986): 605.

14 K.H. Cooper, *Dr Kenneth H. Cooper's Antioxidant Revolution.*

15 H. Franke, *Auf den Spuren der Langlebigkeit.*

16 C.M. McCay, M.F. Crowell, and L.A. Maynard, 'The effects of retarded growth upon the length of life span and upon the ultimate body size', *Journal of Nutrition* 10 (1935): 63–79; C.M. McCay, G.H. Ellis, L.L. Barnes, C.A.H. Smith, and G. Sperling, 'Chemical and pathological changes in aging and after retarded growth', *Journal of Nutrition* 18 (1939): 15–25.

17 R. Walford and S. R. Spindler, 'The response to caloric restriction in mammals shows features also common to hibernation: a cross-adaptation hypothesis', *Journal of Gerontology: Biological Sciences* 52 (1997): B179 – B183.

18 H. Franke, *Auf den Spuren der Langlebigkeit.*

19 H. Franke, *Auf den Spuren der Langlebigkeit.*

20 R.B. Effros, R.L. Walford, R. Weindruch, and C. Mitcheltree, 'Influence of dietary restriction on immunity to influenza in aged mice', *Journal of Gerontology: Biological Sciences* 46, 4 (1991): B142 – B147.

21 Prof. Dr Rolf Schulte-Herrmann conducted several studies on calorie restriction and carcinogenesis.

22 V. Worthington, 'Nutritional quality of organic versus conventional fruits, vegetables, and grains', *Journal of Alternative and Complementary Medicine* 7, 2 (April 2001): 161–173.

23 *Die Welt,* 6 December 2000.

24 R. Walford, *Maximum Life Span.*

25 D. Rudman, et al., 'Effects of human growth hormone in men over sixty years old', *The New England Journal of Medicine* 323 (July 1990): 1–5.

26 J. Huber and A. Worm, *Länger Leben, Später Altern* (Vienna, Austria: Verlag für medizinische Wissenschaft Wilhelm Maudrich, 1998), 286.

27 R. Walford, *Maximum Life Span*.

28 Accessed on the BeliefNet website on 18 July 2003: www.beliefnet.com/features/fasting_chart.html.

29 K.M. Flegal, et al., 'The influence of smoking cessation on the prevalence of overweight in the United States', *New England Journal of Medicine* 333 (1995): 1165–1170.

30 L. Hodel and P. J. Grob, 'Abteilung f. klinische Immunologie, Universitätsspital Zürich,' *Schweizerische Medizinische Wochenschrift*, 123, 49 (1993): 2323–2341.

31 'Arteriosklerose durch Stress und Depressionen', *Die Welt*, 29 April 2000.

32 T.H. Holmes and M. Masuda, 'Life change and illness susceptibility', presented at the Symposium on Separation and Depression; Clinical and Research Aspects, Chicago, 1970. T.H. Holmes and M. Masuda, 'Holmes-Rahe life changes scale', *Journal of Psychomatic Research* 11 (1967), 213–218.

33 P. Wilson, *Instant Calm: Over 100 Easy-to-Use Techniques for Relaxing Mind and Body* (New York: Plume, 1999). [Information appears on p. 27 of the German edition, *Wege zur Ruhe*.]

34 Accessed on Blue Cross and Blue Shield of Texas's website on 18 July 2003: www.bcbstx.com/health/articles/200212_pets.htm.

35 P. Axt and H. Fuch, *Die Wandlungskraft des positiven Denkens* (Fulda, Germany: Paidia Verlag, 1994).

36 O.C. Simonton, S. Mathews-Simonton, and J.L. Creighton, *Getting Well Again* (New York: Bantam Books, 1992).

37 K. Spiegel, R. Leproult, and E. Van Cauter, 'Impact of sleep debt on metabolic and endocrine function', *Lanset* 354, 9188 (1999): 1435.

38 C. Angela, et al., 'Why early means surly', *New Scientist* [UK] (4 November 1999).

39 R. Epstein, N. Chillag, and P. Lavie, 'Starting times of school: effects on daytime functioning of fifth-grade children in Israel', *Sleep* 21, 3 (1998): 250–256.

40 More information on Frankl and his theories can be found on psychology websites such as: www.student.lu.se/~tps97arv/termin4/perspsyk/ovrigt/psykolog/frankl.html.

41 R. Eisner, 'Go to Sleep'. Article accessed on ABCNews.com website on 18 July 2003.

42 D. Schrader, 'Sunlight'. Review of *Sunlight Could Save Your Life*, by Zane R. Kime, *Nude & Natural* 10.1 (1990): 98. Accessed on the Internet: http://cheef.com/buffaloskin/Answers/The_Pro_Con/205Reasons/Credits/credits.html.

43 The website http://bluthochdruck.msd.de/vorbeugen/posi_2200.html summarises the results of a study conducted by the Free University of Berlin ('Biopositive Wirkungen von UV-Strahlung') about the positive effects of sunlight on blood pressure.

44 Z.R. Kine. *Sunlight* (Penryn, CA: World Health Publications, 1980).

45 I. Axt and P. Axt, *Fitness und Gesundheit* (Ravensburg, Germany: Ravensburger Verlag, 1984).

46 Consumer.gov, a resource for consumer information sponsored by the U.S. federal government. Accessed on the Internet: www.consumer.gov/weightloss/bmi.htm.

Index

About the authors

Peter Axt PhD, a former leading member of the German Track and Field Association, is a health scientist and has written several books and numerous essays in medical journals.

Michaela Axt-Gadermann is a doctor, journalist, and the author of several books and medical journal articles.

Both authors live and work in Germany.

Further titles from Bloomsbury reference

Deal with stress: How to take control of your work (Steps to Success series)
ISBN 0–7475–7204–6

While it's said that a little stress is good for you, too much can damage your health, your performance at work, and your relationships. Stress is now part of everyday life, with constant demands for 'more, quicker, and better' increasing the pressure.

Deal with stress offers practical solutions and advice on combating stress and reaching good work/life balance. It will help you to understand the causes, identify the symptoms, and find the right answers for you.

Balance your life and work: How to get the best from your job and still have a life (Steps to Success series)
ISBN 0–7475–7738–2

There's so much pressure on many people today to succeed at work that sometimes, 'real life' tends to take a backseat. Your relationships with friends, family, partner, and children can all suffer as you try to cram everything into a normal day.

If you feel overwhelmed by the constant juggling of different areas of your life, this book can help. It offers sound, easy-to-read, and practical advice on how to regain your equilibrium and keep work in its place. It will help you work out your own priorities, reduce your stress levels, and take positive action to make your life easier.

Get the best from a career break: How to make the most of your time away from the office (Steps to Success series)
ISBN 0–7475–7739–0

A must-read for anyone thinking about time out from the office, this book covers all the key issues you need to think about, from working out your priorities, to assessing your financial situation, to planning the best career break option for you.

Whether you're hankering after the gap year you never took, you have new family responsibilities, or you want to pursue a long-held dream, taking a career break can give you the time and space you need. *Get the best from a career break* offers you practical advice that will make even the most tentative plans a reality.

Manage your time: How to work more effectively (Steps to Success series)
ISBN 0–7475–7206–2

So many e-mails, so little time to read them . . . Life at work has never been busier than it is today, and it is easy to become swamped by Post-It notes, half-written messages, and reminders of meetings you've forgotten about.

Manage Your Time provides structured advice on how to take back control of your desk and prioritise your work so that you have more time for your social life.